C000246431

Jonah, the Reluctant Missionary

Jonah, the Reluctant Missionary

D. Peter Burrows

GRACEWING

First published in 2008 by

Gracewing
2 Southern Avenue,
Leominster
Herefordshire HR6 0QF

All rights reserved. No part of this publication may be reproduced, stored in a retrieval system, or transmitted in any form, or by any means, electronic, mechanical, photo-copying, recording or otherwise, without the written permission of the publisher.

© D. Peter Burrows 2008

The right of D. Peter Burrows to be identified as the author of this work has been asserted in accordance with the Copy-right, Designs and Patents Act 1988.

ISBN 978 085244 652 2

Cover picture © Chris McDonnell, with grateful thanks from the author

Typeset by Action Publishing Technology Ltd,
Gloucester GL1 5SR

When the crowds were increasing, he began to say, 'This generation is an evil generation; it asks for a sign, but no sign will be given to it except the sign of Jonah.'
(Luke 11:29)

Thus says the Lord of hosts: In those days ten men from the nations of every tongue shall take hold of the coat-tail of a Jew, saying, 'Let us go with you, for we have heard that God is with you'.
(Zechariah 8:23)

Contents

Acknowledgements   ix

Chapter One   1
Chapter Two   49
Chapter Three   89
Chapter Four   128
Chapter Five   145

Acknowledgements

This book is dedicated to the Society of African Missions (SMA) and particularly to the British Province of that Society whose hospitality I have enjoyed for many years.

The SMA are not reluctant missionaries; since they began their proclamation of repentance and the gospel of God's mercy these men have been marked also by the kind of self-sacrifice discussed in this book which characterizes true suffering servants of the Lord.

The first Founder of the Society, Bishop Melchior de Brésillac and six companions founded the Society on the Feast of the Immaculate Conception, 1856. They arrived in Sierra Leone on 14 May 1859, and a little over a month later all but one had given their lives for their mission in an outbreak of yellow fever.

Undaunted in their zeal for Africa and the command of the Lord, 'Get up and go into all the world and preach', the second Founder, Augustine Planque, reorganized the Society and made it possible for Brésillac's vision to survive and then flourish. Since then, these enthusiastic missionaries have continued preaching just as the Lord commanded Jonah so long ago. And they have made that sacrifice of their lives, families and goods in accordance with the priestly formula: 'Take me, bind me and throw me overboard; all of this is Your set purpose, O Lord'. They have made the storm pass for thousands and replaced fear with faith throughout the continent of Africa. God is well-served by these servants who continue to redeem His world for Him.

This book is also *in memoriam* of the Missionary Institute London whose closure in June, 2007 signals the fulfilment of a remarkable missionary undertaking in the training and education of missionaries. Its history is a success story of great note. It was my privilege to teach at the 'MIL' during its latter days and I am gratified that its work continues, now in Africa and other places of missionary training throughout the world where that work now properly belongs.

Finally this book is in thanksgiving for my special 'family' by whose love, support and encouragement I have been nurtured and sustained in my own somewhat kaleidoscopic mission. Thank you Rob, Michael and Dermot, my brothers in Christ! Blessings on my little ones, Tia, Carrie and theirs. And on my teachers, Peace.

Chapter One

As a twelve-year-old Baptist Sunday School student, I recall my teacher spending three Sunday sessions exploring the kinds of fish in the Mediterranean Sea with throats large enough to swallow a man, apropos the prophet Jonah. After three weeks, she was frustrated; but I was hooked on the mystery!

Now, after studying and teaching this little book for fifty-five years, I am beginning to understand that when Jesus said in Matthew 12:39–41[1] that he would give his generation of Israelites only one more sign, the sign of Jonah, he was indicating something well beyond a three-day sojourn in death as signified by Jonah's three days in the great fish.

Certainly Jesus does intend his words to refer to his coming days in the grave, for he makes the clear parallel in Matthew 12:39:

> Jonah was in the sea-monster's belly for three days and three nights, and in the same way the Son of Man will be three days and three nights in the bowels of the earth.[2]

---

1 cf. Matt. 16:4 and Luke 11:29–32.
2 More about this further on.

Yet beyond this single verse, Jesus' reference to Jonah is not about the fish, but about the Gentile mission of the prophet and the preference of God for repentance over national arrogance, national prejudice and pride in 'chosenness'.

I am convinced, furthermore, that there is an even more powerful meaning to the 'sign of Jonah' which is related to Jesus' use of the words 'son of man' in reference to himself and related to the same words speaking of his own sacrifice on the cross in Luke 18:31–4.[3] I believe that this meaning is connected with Jesus' understanding of himself as the Messiah, Son of Aaron, the High Priest of Israel and the sacrifice of the atonement.[4]

For a clearer understanding of these three themes we must examine this little Book of Jonah carefully and in its entirety. But first we must recognize the manner in which we understand the truth of Jonah as the Word of God.

While the measure of truth in our Western world tends to be scientific and thus subject to provability, we must be clear that for the ancients in general and the Bible in particular, science and the scientific method are of almost no concern. This significant difference between our mindset and the biblical mindset arises primarily out of our preference for nouns and things over their preference for verbs and actions. And this is due to a clear deficiency in Semitic thought and language of a present tense of the verb 'to be'. Modern thought is much influenced by the Greek mindset which is rich in words for being and essence. Thus we can and do speak of the being of things and the analysis of that being by science. To know the 'truth' of something is to be able to analyse it and to prove it.

Not so Semitic thought. Ancient Hebrew and its related languages make nouns out of verb stems and discern the truth by participating in the action. A pencil and a pen are not different by reason of the use of wood, plastic, graphite

---

3 cf. Mark 10:32–4 and Matt. 20:17–19.
4 See my article 'The Relationship between the Passover and the Mass: Catholic and Protestant Understandings' in *Faith*, Vol. 39, No. 3, May–June 2007, pp. 16–20.

or ink in their composition as would be true for us. A pen and a pencil are the same in the Semitic mind set because they both write – the action is critical.

This difference extends to our acceptance of history as a measure of the truth. If it is provable historically (through archaeology, carbon dating, literary studies and the like) we would say that it is true. By extension, then, we measure the reliability and the truth of the Bible by its historical provability. Otherwise, we call it 'a myth' and suggest that it is not really true. Time and place are everything, even though the Bible makes it clear that God created place and time on the third and fourth 'days' of creation – and that God and His Truth stand before the beginning.

For Semitic thought, history and science are of no consideration in the demonstration of truth. The truth is in the verb and in what happens; the biblical record is an account of what happens between God and his creation, his people and the peoples of the world. This measure of truth is always verifiable at any particular time and place by any individual, for the God-experience is always the same. God is always creating and making whole; humankind is always engaged in choosing to work with God or against Him. And God's plan, his programme, revealed at the beginning will be the same at the end and at all times and in all places. This is the truth and is as verifiable for me in my life as it was for my grandsires and will be for my grandchildren.

The form of literature which expresses truth in this way is called a parable. Parables are always true and in all places because the truth is in the action of them and not the characters. Jesus makes this clear when he says: 'The Kingdom of Heaven is like what *happens* in the case of thus and so.' In the parable of the Prodigal Son, it is clear that the prodigal and his jealous older brother bear our own names, mine and yours. Here is no historical story – rather it is our own story, each one of us.

Perhaps this is a rather longish way of saying that the Book of Jonah is a parable. There is no point in trying to date the prophet or to know about his personal details – or to determine the kind of big fish in the story. The Bible doesn't give a fig! We may use a standard formula for the beginning of a parable: 'Once upon a time ...'

I. 1 [*Once upon a time*] *the Word of the Lord came to Jonah son of Amittai, to wit:*

Jonah son of Amittai is mentioned only in 2 Kings 14:25 in conjunction with a decision the Lord had come to regarding his first intention of destroying the kingdom of Israel without leaving a remnant for the future at the time of the wicked king Jeroboam II. In short, the Lord had changed his mind, and through the word of Jonah promised a remnant would remain. We know, then, that Jonah is a prophet of the northern kingdom of Israel and we are introduced to the problem of this parable: Why does God change his mind and leave a remnant of Israel in the world?[5] The question is the same in all the other examples of remnants that we find in Scripture, for example the remnant of the family of Israel in bondage in Egypt, the remnant of the kingdom of Judah after the destruction of the Temple by

---

5 That the overthrow of the northern kingdom of Israel was the same trauma and raised the same questions as the later overthrow of Jerusalem by the Babylonians is suggested in the following little extract from the Book of 2 Esdras: 'Then he, my Son, will reprove the assembled nations for their ungodliness (this was symbolized by the storm), and will reproach them to their face with their evil thoughts and the torments with which they are to be tortured (which were symbolized by the flames), and will destroy them without effort by means of the law (which was symbolized by the fire). And as for your seeing him gather to himself another multitude that was peaceable, these are the nine tribes that were taken away from their own land into exile in the days of King Hoshea, whom Shalmaneser, king of the Assyrians, made captives; he took them across the river, and they were taken into another land. But they formed this plan for themselves, that they would leave the multitude of the nations and go to a more distant region, where no human beings had ever lived, so that there at least they might keep their statutes that they had not kept in their own land. And they went in by the narrow passages of the Euphrates river.' (2 Esdras 13:37–43).

King Nebuchadnezzar and finally the righteous remnant that we find after the great destruction in the Book of Revelation at the end of the Bible.

There is already a clue to the 'sign of Jonah' in Jonah's name. The Bible loves puns, word plays and especially puns on names. The name of the character suggests the purpose or function of the character. Jonah's name means 'dove' in Hebrew; we are meant to associate this with the dove that appeared to Noah after the great storm of destruction in the Flood. The dove was, in the parable of Noah, the sign of the end of the chaos and the re-creation of the world. It was a sign too of Noah's salvation. We are perhaps also invited to think of pigeons such as those flocking in St Mark's Square in Venice. When they are alarmed, they fly off in every direction, feathers flying, much as we will see Jonah trying to 'fly' away from the Lord's presence.

Perhaps most important of all, however, in the pun rendered by Jonah's name is the designation in the Book of Leviticus of the 'jonah,' or turtledove as a possible substitute for those who cannot afford a lamb as an atonement sacrifice for sin, especially the sin of dealing with uncleanness or making false oaths or vows. Clearly, a 'jonah' is an atonement sacrifice for sin.

> When you realize your guilt in any of these, you shall confess the sin that you have committed. And you shall bring to the Lord, as your penalty for the sin that you have committed, a female from the flock, a sheep or a goat, as a sin offering; and the priest shall make atonement on your behalf for your sin. But if you cannot afford a sheep, you shall bring to the Lord, as your penalty for the sin that you have committed two turtledoves or two pigeons, one for a sin offering and the other for a burnt offering. You shall bring them to the priest, who shall offer first the one for the sin offering, wringing its head at the nape without severing it. He shall sprinkle some of the blood of the sin offering on the side of the altar, while the rest of the blood shall be drained out at the base of the altar; it is a sin offering.[6]

6 Lev. 5:5–9.

I. 2 *'Get up and go to that great city of Nineveh and summon it [to repentance]: for their wickedness has come to My attention!'*

The formula 'The Word of the Lord came and said, "Get up and go, and leave ...!"' is significant. It was this very formula by which God addressed Abraham in Ur of the Chaldees when he called him to leave his Gentile ways and to become the beginnings of the people of God. 'Repent of your former life among the nations and return to the Lord God, for he wishes to save you'. The final commission of Jesus to his disciples at his Ascension begins with the same formula: '[Get up and] go into all the nations and preach the Gospel [of repentance and salvation] to all peoples!' Here it is clear that Jonah's mission is to go to the Gentiles, the 'people of uncleanness', and preach repentance to them. His 'cry' is to be a summons to repent, not a condemnation. John 3:16–17 is the same:

> God so loved *the world* that he gave his only-begotten Son, so that all who believe him will not die but have eternal life. It was not to condemn the world that God sent his Son into the world, but that through him the nations might be saved.

God's will to save through repentance is clear here, as is the will that salvation be extended to all peoples, the nations of the world, the unclean Gentiles who have made vows to gods of uncleanness.

By naming Nineveh as the mission field, another problem of this parable is revealed. Nineveh, the capital of the empire of Assyria, becomes the arch-enemy of the little kingdom of Israel. When the king of Assyria led his armies against Israel, the conquest was a particularly brutal one, quite barbaric and destructive. Few prisoners were taken and entire families were obliterated. If one were an Israelite, as Jonah was, we might not be surprised at the objection: 'These barbarians do not deserve to be saved!' 'Why should I go to the destroyers of my family and people so that they might be saved? And why me?' 'Where is the justice in this? – that's not fair!'

It is possible that this parable of Jonah is like the parable of Job in this question concerning the justice of God. The parable of Job is really the story of the destruction of Jerusalem and Judah and the question that arises from this destruction: If God is good and just and we are the faithful and chosen people of God, why does God allow this monstrous injustice to befall his elect? We call this problem 'theodicy' – the problem of the justice of God in the face of apparent evil. Job becomes so distraught over this that he begins to say: 'I would rather die than live in a universe where God is unjust!' The resolution of the problem in Job and in Jonah will, in fact, be the same.

I. 3 *Jonah, however, got up and ran for Tarshish to escape the Lord's presence. He went down to Joppa and found a ship going to Tarshish. He paid the fare and went aboard to sail with the others to Tarshish, away from the Word of the Lord.*

Jonah, like Israel generally, believed that God's Word was only spoken and discerned in God's own land. The northern kingdom of Israel conceived of the Lord as enthroned upon the entire land with the armrests of his throne at the shrines at the northern and southern borders of the land. God's Word spoken from his throne was only available in the land itself.[7] If one could escape the land, God's very Word could be avoided! Tarshish is clearly neutral territory and void of the divine imperative. One is tempted to note the similarity of Tarshish with Tarsus, home of St Paul, the missionary to the Gentiles. Certainly there is a kind of foreboding of storms on the journey to Tarshish:

As soon as they saw it, they were astounded; they were in

---

7 In the kingdom of Judah, the Lord's throne was in the Holy of Holies in the Temple, the mercy-seat of the Ark of the Covenant being his throne and the armrests being the two cherubim on the Ark. Thus the Temple in Jerusalem was the centralization of the divine Presence, while the land itself was the temple in Israel.

panic, they took to flight; trembling took hold of them
there, pains as of a woman in labour, as when an east wind
shatters the ships of Tarshish.[8]

Some commentators on this passage opine that Jonah's
decision to run from God's Word is motivated by fear, that
is, his fear of going to the city of the enemy. This is surely a
mistake as we shall see further along. If Jonah is afraid at
all, he fears that if he preaches to the enemy and urges them
to repentance for their wickedness, they might indeed
repent. Then what is unthinkable might happen – God
might save them and spare them from what Jonah believes
is their richly-deserved punishment.

Joppa is the likely seaport for sea travel from Israel. In
the Book of Acts, it was at Joppa that St Peter had his great
vision of the bedsheet with the unclean food and was finally
convinced of the Gentile mission of the Church, much to his
chagrin. Perhaps this is why Jesus addresses him several
times as Simon son of Jonah (John 1:42; 21:15–17).

I. 4 *But the Lord hurled a mighty wind upon the sea, and such a great storm came upon the sea that the ship was in danger of breaking up.*

While such major storms are not infrequent in the Mediterranean, we must here remember that this is a parable, and
this storm is but a single example of mighty storms throughout Scripture. Furthermore, as we shall see in the next verse,
it is not a normal storm in which sailors first batten down
the hatches to meet it; this is so great a storm that experi-
enced sailors cry out to their gods first. This tempest must
be described properly as 'all hell breaking loose'.

We are first introduced to this kind of storm at the beginning of the Bible, in Genesis 1:2:

Now the earth was [at first] nothing more than a formless
mass, steeped in total darkness and a mighty divine wind

8 Ps. 48:5–7.

whipping aimlessly over the face of the waters of the deep.

It was into this chaos that God introjected his divine Word, a pattern of Order that first divided this from that; then named the one (light) and the opposite (dark), thus giving them value and 'reality'; and then put them in balance with each other ('and the light shone in the darkness, and the darkness never overwhelmed it'[9]). The Word of God creates Order out of the Chaos which the Bible understands as the real hell. Without God's Word all hell breaks loose, and the tendency of all creation, deprived of God's Word, is to go back inexorably to the disordered hell from which it came. Without God's sustaining Word, the world breaks down and falls apart.

Furthermore, it is only in the ordered creation that life itself can flourish, for later in the creation parable, when God introduces life on the fifth and sixth days, he blesses it and makes it the fundamental principle and gift in creation: 'God blessed it and said, "Let it flow on forever unhampered!"'[10] Life, then, is at the heart of creation and is only threatened with chaos or hell. Death is the driving force of the chaos and is the antithesis of God's life-giving Word.

In the story of Noah later on, the chaos – the Flood – returns. It comes because:

> The Lord saw how great was man's wickedness on earth, and how every plan devised by mankind's mind was nothing but evil all the time. And the Lord bitterly regretted that he had made humankind on the earth.[11]

So God withdrew his Word from the earth and the whole thing collapsed. Yet Noah and his household were spared, and this was because Noah was a righteous man, that is, he behaved according to the Word of God. Noah is given a little world, the Ark which was modelled on the larger one

9 John 1:5.
10 Gen. 1:22.
11 Gen. 6:5–6.

in which to live while the rest of creation is allowed to melt down to its fundamental chaos. Only when the restoration and renewal of creation is complete after forty days is this son of Adam delivered from the floods of the deep and allowed to return to a renewed creation, together with the living creatures with him that were in the Ark. One man has saved the human experiment by his righteousness. A son of man has saved the human species, so to speak; one human has saved the whole of humanity. Noah may be thought of as the 'righteous remnant' who brings salvation from the flood.

Certainly the city from which Abraham departs when God says to him, 'Get up and go!' is described as a place of chaos and the storm of the conflict of languages and cultures, none of which know the Lord and his Word. Babylon is a babble and confusion. And out of this chaos of 'civilization', God calls Abraham.

The same is true of the land of Egypt in which the people of Israel have lost their definition and their status as a people. Egypt is described as a place of meltdown over which one man, Pharaoh, has claimed to be the king and god. Pharaoh's word extends over the whole of Egypt and the Word of God is non-existent. Egypt is a place of bondage and death, a hell of a place! Moses hears the Word of God in the wilderness on Sinai, a word which says to him: 'Get up and go and bring my people out of Egypt.' For forty years they are in the wilderness, learning the Word of God so that they might be able to live in the Promised Land, the kingdom where God is king and his Word holds sway, the kingdom of heaven.

We encounter this parable of the storm in the descriptions of the destruction of Jerusalem and Judah by the Babylonians. Though the prophets have persistently called on the people to return to the Word of God and by their repentance to be saved from the pending chaos and hell, yet the people will not listen and the nation is allowed by God to collapse in the flood of the armies of Nebuchadnezzar. The Lord, however, does not want the entire experiment of

Israel to end altogether, and so we hear of a righteous remnant that is spared as a seed of the renewed Israel, just as in the case of Noah.[12]

The figures of Jeremiah and Job become the characterizations of this remnant, the suffering servants of God.[13] They raise the major question of the storm – why does it happen and why does God save a remnant to go into exile? Can it be fair that the righteous should suffer? And if not fair, then why? When all hell breaks loose, is there a larger purpose to the sufferings of Israel, God's own people?

The storm of Jonah returns in Mark 4:35–41. Again it is a case of all hell breaking loose, and those in the boat are in fear of their lives and do not know how to save themselves. It is as though Jesus is showing his disciples the state of the world which does not know of God and his Word – for he is asleep in the middle of the chaos as though he did not care. They wake him in their fear, and he speaks the Word to the chaos – 'Peace! Be still!' – and the order of creation is restored.

That the storm motif is crucial to the 'sign of Jonah' as Jesus invokes it becomes clear in the events around the cross:

> From midday a darkness fell over the whole land, which lasted until three in the afternoon; and about three Jesus cried out, '*Eli, Eli, lamah sabachthani?*' Which means, 'My God, my God, why hast thou forsaken me?'
>
> There was an earthquake, the rocks split and the graves opened, and many of God's saints were raised from sleep; and coming out of their graves after his resurrection they entered the holy city, where many saw them. And when the Roman (gentile) centurion and his men who were keeping watch over Jesus saw the earthquake and all that was happening, they were filled with fear, and they cried, 'Truly this man was a son of God!'[14]

---

12 See, for example, Isa. 10:21–2.
13 See particularly Jer. 20:7ff and Job 3 and 19.
14 Matt. 27:45f and 51b–54. cf. Mark 15:33f; Luke 23:44ff.

All hell breaks loose around the cross, the very chaos in which a godless world finds itself and is terrified of death. Once more, the Word of God is introjected into the chaos: 'Peace! Be still!' 'It is finished!' The whole of creation is restored and made new. The son of man, this new Adam, is taken down from the cross. God rests on the Sabbath. And on the first day of the week, the Word thunders: 'Light!' And there is light. And this time it is, as in the days of Noah, for all peoples rather than a chosen few.

Finally we meet the storm of hell and chaos at the end of the Bible in the florid vision of the end of all things in Revelation 14–20. The breaking loose of all hell is described in detail and the horror and fear of it is graphically portrayed. The remnant, here 144 thousand plus a vast multitude of those signed with God's special mark, are protected like Noah of old from the floods of destruction. The Son of Man makes a final appearance and utters his familiar: 'Do not be afraid!'[15] He is the servant who has suffered and who was dead and is now alive.[16]

The destruction is complete and only the righteous remnant have survived. Then we are given a vision of the renewed creation:

> Then I saw a new heaven and a new earth, for the first heaven and the first earth had vanished, and there was no longer any sea. I saw the holy city, new Jerusalem, coming down out of heaven from God, made ready like a bride adorned for her husband.
>
> Then he who sat on the throne said, 'Behold! I am making all things new!'[17]

15 Rev. 1:13–19.
16 Rev. 1:7 cf. Zech. 12:10 and Rev. 1:17f.
17 Rev. 21:1–3; 5.

I. 5 *And the sailors were so overcome with fear that each one called to his own deity; and then they began to throw the ship's cargo into the sea to make it lighter for them. Meanwhile, Jonah had gone down into the hold of the ship where he lay down and went to sleep.*

We have already noted that the normal course of sailors in a regular storm is to 'batten down the hatches' first, and only then, if necessary, to resort to prayer; do the best you can first and then ask for help. Here the order is reversed, suggesting the enormity of the storm – a hell of a storm indeed. It is noteworthy that in their prayers they call out to their own gods, suggesting that these sailors are what would be thought of as Gentiles, not knowing the Lord God. The gods of the nations cannot help them and so they must resort to saving themselves. Notice, too, the great fear that overwhelms the crew. The bottom line of all fear is the fear of death. We might say they are 'scared to (of) death'.

Even our smallest fears have their roots in our mortality and our ultimate inability to keep ourselves alive. The real problem of the world is not sin; it is fear of death without remedy. Thus Jesus says more times in the Gospels 'Do not be afraid' than he even says to 'love one another'. He knows the real problem of those caught up in the storms and hells of life. The sailors are terrified because their gods are of no use and their own efforts at keeping themselves alive are to no avail.

As suggested above, this same terror afflicts the disciples who are out in the boat with Jesus when the storm comes upon them. It is as though Jesus, in order to prepare them for their mission in the world, wants them to endure the same terror that afflicts all peoples who do not know the Lord God. Surely, personal experience leads to deeper understanding and compassion.

Where is Jonah – and Jesus – in the midst of this catastrophe of chaos? Both are lying down in the boat, *asleep!* It is as though neither Jonah nor Jesus is concerned or afraid at all. Their sleep is compared and contrasted to the others' fear of death and makes us wonder what they know that the sailors/disciples do not. Wherein lies the difference, for they seem to be sure of their safety and peace? We get the feeling from this sleeping of Jonah and Jesus: 'I'm OK, Jack, and it's a shame about you! Stay warm and well-fed!'

I. 6 *The captain came over to him and cried out, 'How can you be sleeping so soundly! Get up and call upon your god! Perhaps the god will show us mercy and we will not die.'*

Even the ruler of the ship (Hebrew calls him 'Rav') is afraid and does not know what to do in this hellish situation and turns to one who is not a member of the ship's company for help. We are reminded here of Pharaoh at the time of the plagues in Egypt who, though he calls himself the god of Egypt, must turn in his fear and insufficiency to Moses for help. But Jonah is asleep! How can anyone be asleep in the face of imminent death? It is a case of 'he must know something we do not know'. 'Sleeper, awake! Get up and do something!' cries the captain to the sleeping Jonah.

In the same way the disciples in the storm turn to Jesus in their panic and alarm. And where is Jesus? Like Jonah he is asleep, on a pillow in the stern of the boat. 'Lord, wake up! Do you not care that we are dying?' The fear of death becomes the opportunity to look beyond ourselves for our salvation. Fear overcomes our pride in being able to manage everything ourselves and drives us to a search for the Almighty.

Clearly the captain is not interested in Jonah personally, but in Jonah's God. 'Get up, and call upon your god!' Perhaps the captain suspects that if Jonah can sleep while all hell is breaking loose he must have a very powerful divine protection. The captain cannot call upon Jonah's God himself simply because he does not know him. The captain and his crew need an intercessor who is familiar enough with Deity and his ways as to call upon him for relief.

The sleeping Jonah is the Jonah who will not go to Nineveh because he believes its people not worthy of salvation. Ninevites are, according to Jonah's judgement, sinners and not fit to hear the Word of God or to be called to repentance lest they do repent and are saved. The anti-Gentile bias of Israel is clear in the tradition, never mind what God desires. The same bias is evident in the encounter of Jesus with the Canaanite woman in Matthew's Gospel:

> A Canaanite woman from the area of Tyre and Sidon came crying out to Jesus: 'Sir! Have pity on me, Son of David; my daughter is tormented by a devil.' But he said not a word in reply. His disciples came and urged him: 'Send her away; see how she comes shouting after us'. Jesus replied, 'I was sent to the lost sheep of the House of Israel, and to them alone.' But the woman came and fell at his feet and begged him: 'Help me, sir!' To this Jesus replied, 'It is not right to take the children's bread and throw it to the dogs.' 'True, sir,' she replied, 'and yet the dogs eat the scraps that fall from their masters' table'. Hearing this, Jesus replied, 'Woman, what faith you have! Be it as you wish!' And from that moment her daughter was restored to health.[18]

It is hard to explain this story in any other way than that Jesus changed his mind as a result of this woman's anxious cry, and extended salvation to a Gentile. We might even say that Jesus repented here, not of sin but in the sense that because of his great humility he could change his mind and choose to act differently. We should note also that it was the woman's faith, her willingness to place her fears in the Lord's hands, which brought salvation.

Again, in Acts 10, we see the Apostle Peter confronted with the same dilemma. Peter was asleep on the roof and in his trance he saw a sailcloth descend from the heavens coming to the ground.

> In it he saw creatures of every kind, whatever walks or crawls or flies. Then there was a voice which said to him,

18 Matt. 15:21–8; cf. Mark 7:24–9.

'Get up, Peter, kill and eat'. But Peter said, 'No, Lord, no. I have never eaten anything profane or unclean.' The voice came a second time: 'It is not for you to call profane what God counts clean'. This happened three times; and then the thing was taken up again into the heavens.[19]

And further along in the same narrative we see that Peter ends up baptizing the Gentiles, having declared: 'I now see how true it is that God has no favourites, but that in every nation that man who is god-fearing and does what is good is acceptable to him'.[20] Peter had been asleep to the terror of the Gentiles and was awakened by his vision.

The captain, upon rousing Jonah, asks him to make intercession in the hope for mercy that will keep them all from dying. He uses the word 'perhaps'. The captain senses what we often forget, that mercy is never to be demanded or required, especially from God; it is always a matter of 'please'. Many Christians begin their liturgies with the formula: 'Lord, have mercy!' Yet rarely do we say, 'Please'. Mercy is a plea to the judge who has found us already at fault – 'Please, Sir, have mercy on me a sinner!' It is 'throwing oneself on the mercy of the court'. The captain of this ship is wiser than we are; he knows that salvation in his situation is only a 'maybe' at best.[21]

I. 7 *The men [of the crew] agreed among themselves, saying, 'Let us cast lots and find out just who might bear responsibility for this disaster which has befallen us'. They cast the lots and the lot fell on Jonah.*

Fear brings about what pride cannot, the agreement of the sailors among themselves. It was the very pride of the men

19 Acts 10:11–16.
20 Acts 10:34f.
21 Christian liturgy admits of only one liturgical word, a Hebrew one, that contains 'please'. Hosan-nah is a combination of *hoshia*, save us and the little particle *na*, please. It is a most salutary word.

of Babylon in building the Tower of Babel to reach and
storm heaven that brought about their confusion and
babbling in different languages. In an opposite way we
might guess that anxiety of Pilate and Herod over Jesus'
possible innocence leads Luke to observe: 'That same day
Herod and Pilate became friends with each other; before
this they had been enemies'.[22]

Some translations of this verse use the word 'fault' in the
sense of 'let us find out whose "fault" this storm is', as
though Jonah were in some way guilty of bringing on the
chaos. The Hebrew word is more convoluted, but in no way
suggests guilt for Jonah. Jonah has committed no sin. Nor
could we imagine that the Lord would punish a whole
people because one of them has sinned.[23] The Latin Vulgate
gives a more generalized translation and is perhaps more
useful than using the word 'blame': 'Let us cast lots so that
we might discover wherefore (*quare*) this evil is upon us.'
The sailors throw the dice to find out just who on board
might know the solution to their impending doom.

In this there is perhaps the deeper meaning, 'Who on
board knows what to do about it?' 'Who will take it on his
own account or take responsibility for it?' Clearly the
sailors want help rather than someone to blame, and they
are looking for someone in a position to take their own hell
upon himself. We shall see that their real desire with the lots
is to find the sacrifice that will take away the threat of
death.

Apart from the Bible, the deity most often giving answers
through the lots is Fortuna, 'Lady Luck'. In another sense,
lots are like tossing a coin to decide who is 'it'. In this case,
there is no presumed deity behind the fall of the coin –
rather, it is an attempt at randomness.

In the biblical narrative, the lots always presume that the

22 Luke 23:12.
23 The only exception is that when in Scripture the King sins, the people
bear the burden of the punishment, as in the case of King David's sin
in taking a census of the people when God prohibited it (2 Sam.
24:6ff).

Lord God stands behind the fall of the dice. Lots are here a quick method of augury and the casting of lots a common way to know the will of the Almighty. In some cases lots are cast for the discernment and separation of one thing from another. The Promised Land was divided amongst the Twelve Tribes by Joshua when the people had crossed over the Jordan to take possession of it. In this case, it was really the Lord himself who expressed his will concerning the land allotments.[24]

There is another use of lots in the Bible that possibly pertains in our parable of Jonah. One feature of the vestments of Aaron, the High Priest of Israel, as commanded in Exodus and Leviticus is the breastplate, a box studded with twelve semi-precious stones representing the Twelve Tribes. The breastplate is hung around Aaron's neck by a golden rope. Inside are carried the two sacred lots, the *Urim* and the *Thummim*, the oracles of decision (-making) for the Israelites which are held at all times over Aaron's heart. Not only are these lots symbolic of the High Priest's oracular status, they also have a most important function in the sacrifice offered on the Day of Atonement.

All the sacrifices established for Israel are secondary to this great sacrifice for sin offered on the Day of Atonement. This sacrifice could only be offered by the High Priest wearing his special vestments as appointed in Exodus; he and his sons were anointed with oil from generation to generation for the purpose of this sacrifice. Aaron was the original Messiah from of old, well before the time of the anointing of kings beginning with Saul and David. This anointing had to do with the sacrifice itself and not the

---

24 The casting of lots by the victors in order to divide up the spoils is used with great irony in Nahum's prophecy about Nineveh as suffering the same fate as Memphis: 'Yet she became an exile, she went into captivity; even her infants were dashed in pieces at the head of every street; lots were cast for her nobles, all her dignitaries were bound in fetters'. Nahum 3:10.

I will address Nahum's prophecy against Nineveh in chapter 5.

establishment of any royal authority. This particular sacrifice was only for the general forgiveness of sin.

While details varied a little over the centuries, the sacrifice by Aaron and his descendants[25] established in the wilderness in the days of the golden calf remained a constant *mandatum* until the destruction of the Second Temple after the time of Jesus. The origins of this most important liturgy are in the wilderness and preceded the setting up either of the Tabernacle or of the Temple.

In Exodus 32, Moses has brought the Israelites from Egypt to Mount Sinai as the Lord had commanded him to do. At the foot of the mountain Moses told the people to remain there and to do nothing while he went up into the mountain to receive further instructions from God. After Moses had been gone awhile and was receiving the tablets of the Law, the people became afraid that he was not coming back. In their fear they decided that they needed a concrete image of the God who had brought them out of Egypt, a graven image of the Lord. Since they had no instructions yet about graven images, they prevailed upon Moses' brother Aaron to construct one for them.

Aaron gathered up their gold jewellery, melted it down and fashioned a bull-calf. Their fear drove them to worship this idol as though it were the Lord, and they kept a feast to the Lord before the idol. This was an unwitting sin, as they as yet had no law concerning it; they did not know what they were doing. Meanwhile, God is distracted from his giving the Law, becomes furious and threatens to obliterate the people from the earth, raising up a new people from Moses.

Into this great storm of the Lord's anger steps Moses himself, gone weak-kneed with fear; and he implores the Lord to wait before carrying out his threat to obliterate the people. In fact, Moses buys some time in order to see if he

---

25 And after King Solomon, the descendants of the High Priest Zadok of Jerusalem, and their later successors among the Hellenized Maccabeans, the Sadducees.

can bring the people back to order. His argument with God[26] takes the form of a suggestion of unjust impatience on the Lord's part. He reasons: 'You have gone to all the trouble of confronting Pharaoh in Egypt, bringing on Egypt all the plagues; you have gone to all the trouble of parting the sea and delivering the people in safety on the other side; you have led them across the wilderness to the holy mountain. And now you intend to wipe them from the face of the earth! What will the Egyptians say about you and your power when they get word of Israel's destruction? Furthermore, what about your promises to the patriarchs about a great nation?' Appealing both to God's justice and his fidelity, Moses succeeds in deferring punishment of the people until he can at least make an intervention. Moses puts God's anger on hold, standing as it were in the breach.

Having temporarily dealt with God's rage, Moses hurries down the mountain back to the encampment of Israel. As he approaches, he hears the rejoicing of the people over the idol they have made. Moses' rage is stirred and he dashes down the tablets of the Law which he is carrying, destroying them at the foot of the mountain. He takes the golden calf, melts it down and grinds it into powder which he puts in the people's drinking water. When the gold next appears after being ingested by the people, they will know what this 'god' really is – human excrement; a nice touch indeed!

Moses turns now on his brother Aaron who is obviously leading the people in their idolatrous worship. 'What did this people do to you that you should have brought such guilt upon them?'[27] Aaron's defence is that the people were afraid and pleaded for the idol as security; he continues by saying that his only involvement was to collect the gold and

---

26 Moses takes a terrible risk by opposing the Lord's will on the people's behalf. It requires a kind of intimate friendship with the Lord shared only by Abraham before this time when Abraham argues with God about destroying the city of Sodom.

27 Exod. 32:21.

melt it down. 'Then,' he says, 'out popped this bull-calf!' 'It wasn't my fault and the entire affair was completely unplanned'.

St Paul, in his Epistle to the Romans, compares this unwitting sin of the idolatry of Israel to the sin of the nations of the world:

> For the wrath of God is revealed from heaven against all ungodliness and unrighteousness of men, who suppress the truth in unrighteousness, because what may be known of God is manifest in them, for God has shown it to them. For since the creation of the world his invisible attributes are clearly seen, being understood by the things that are made, even his eternal power and Godhead, so that they are without excuse, because, although they knew God, they did not glorify him as God, nor were thankful, but became futile in their thoughts, and their foolish hearts were darkened. Professing to be wise, they became fools, and changed the glory of the incorruptible God into an image made like corruptible man – and birds and four-footed animals and creeping things. Therefore God also gave them up to uncleanness, in the lusts of their hearts, to dishonour their bodies among themselves, who exchanged the truth of God for the lie, and worshipped and served the creature rather than the Creator, who is blessed forever. Amen.[28]

Moses gathers to himself his tribal brethren the Levites, crying out: 'Who is on the Lord's side?' He sends the Levites out with swords into the whole camp from end to end to restore justice and righteousness to the people, who have become a chaos.[29] Moses makes it clear to the Levites that they are to act with strict objectivity, making no allowances for kinsmen or friends. Because of their strict objectivity in

---

28 Rom. 1:18–25.
29 We are here reminded of Jesus' own Levitical statement, 'I have come not to bring peace, but a sword'. Matt. 10:34. The sword in ancient times is the symbol of justice, for with it a case is cut open to discern the right from the wrong.

this judgement, the Levites consecrate themselves as the priestly judges of Israel. They will not own land nor offer an inheritance to their sons – they are to become the Lord's special portion from this time forward and are to live off the offerings and tithes of the people.[30]

The next day Moses announces to the people that they have committed 'a great sin'[31] and that he, Moses, would have to go back to the Lord (whose anger is still only on hold) to make it right. He uses the word 'perhaps' when speaking about the Lord's forgiveness and mercy.

> Moses went back to the Lord and said, 'Alas, this people are guilty of a great sin in making themselves a god of gold. Now, if you will forgive them, please forgive them [they were afraid and didn't know what they were doing]; but if you will not forgive them, wipe my name from the Book which you have written [take my life in the stead of theirs!].' But the Lord said to Moses, 'He who has sinned against me, him only will I erase from the Book'.[32]

Moses' argument to the Lord is that the people have committed an unwitting sin due to their fear. He proposes the formula of vicarious atonement, 'I offer my life in the stead of theirs'. His willingness to die, so that the people do not have to, becomes the standard formula for the atonement offering. The offerer, because he is willing to make this ultimate sacrifice, is designated the suffering servant, that is, he suffers or allows his life to be taken on behalf of

---

30 It is interesting that in Jesus' own day the Levites were ignored concerning the tithe. Since they could not own land and make a living, it is small wonder that Matthew the Levite had to become a tax collector to make his living, a position from which Jesus called him to join with him.

31 I would suggest that this sin of idolatry out of fear (a lack of faith) is, for Israel the Original or Fundamental Sin. Perhaps it is for Christianity as well.

32 Exod. 32:31–33. Clearly Moses is here offering his life for the people's, just the reverse of the Lord's initial statement, 'I will wipe this people out and make a new people arise from you, Moses.'

others.[33] The Lord approves of the formula but rejects
Moses as the sacrifice, indicating that it is Aaron who will
make the offering for sin. At this point, Aaron becomes the
High Priest. He is anointed (Exod. 29:7–8) and becomes the
'messiah', the anointed one who offers his life for the sins of
the people and restores the relationship annually with the
Lord. He and his sons are promised the High Priesthood
forever in Numbers:

> The Lord spoke to Moses, saying, 'Phineas, son of Eleazar,
> son of Aaron the [high] priest, has turned back my wrath
> from the Israelites by displaying among them his passion
> (zeal) for me, so that I did not wipe out the Israelite people
> in my passion. Say, therefore, "I grant him my covenant of
> security of tenure. It shall be for him and for his descendants
> after him a covenant of [high] priesthood for all time,
> because he took zealous action for his God, thus making
> atonement for the Israelites"'.[34]

Since this covenant with the anointed one, the messiah, is
made hundreds of years before the covenant with David
and his house, and since the covenant with David was

---

33 This formula crops up in the Book of Job, which the High Priest is
    required to read on the night before the Day of Atonement (Job 42:8b
    – 'I will reward your suffering, Job, by saving your foreign friends'.
    Some reward!)

34 Num. 25:10–13. We are reminded of Jesus' saying in John 2:17
    (quoting Ps 69:9): 'Zeal for your House has consumed me'. 'Zeal',
    often translated 'jealousy' is here used as enthusiastic preference,
    dedication and focus rather than the anger of Cain for his brother.
    The great and early commentary on the Book of Exodus, the *Mekilta
    de-Rabbi Ishmael*, comments on three kinds of prophets, according
    to their zeal. Elijah is held up as the example of the prophet who is
    more zealous for the Father (God) than for the son (Israel); Jonah, on
    the other hand, is the model of the prophet who is more zealous for
    the son (Israel and its rights) than for the Father (God and His
    Purposes); Jeremiah is praised as equally zealous for the Father and
    the son. (*Mekilta de-Rabbi Ishmael*, Vol. 1, Tractate Pisḥa pp. 8ff.
    Jacob Z. Lauterbach. Jewish Publication Society of America,
    Philadelphia, 1933.)

limited, after Solomon, to only two of Israel's tribes, Judah
and Benjamin, it is evident that Israel's tradition of the high
priestly sacrifice for sin was ever the more important
messianic office than that of a war-leader, which is why
God warned the people that they would not like kings when
they got them, and this before the time of the election of
Saul, the first king.[35]

Zechariah the prophet, in the days preceding Israel's
return from the Exile in the land of the Medes and Persians,
is quite conscious of two messiahs, one a domestic, political
and civic leader (though never again a king until the
Maccabean king/priests and the Herodians) and the other
the High Priest:

> Then I said to him, 'What are these two olive trees on the
> right and the left of the lampstand?' And a second time I
> said to him, 'What are these two branches of the olive trees,
> which pour out the oil through the two golden pipes?' He
> said to me, 'Do you not know what these are?' I said, 'No,
> my lord'. Then he said, 'These are the two anointed ones
> who stand by the Lord of the whole earth'.[36]

The Church from earliest times was keen to find in Jesus the
fulfilment of all the promises made by God to his people. It
would be strange, then, to find this covenant with the
House of Aaron concerning the anointed High Priesthood
overlooked. It is important to note that this covenant was
not with the priesthood of Melchizedek, the High Priest
whom Solomon installed in his new temple in Jerusalem

---

35 In fact, during the time of the judges and well before Saul the issue of
    kingship had arisen when the judge Gideon, who had been successful
    as a military leader against the Midianites, was offered and even
    urged to become the king of Israel. He refused the kingship quite
    firmly: 'Then the Israelites said to Gideon, "Rule over us, you and
    your son and your grandson also; for you have delivered us out of the
    hand of Midian". Gideon said to them, "I will not rule over you, and
    my son will not rule over you; the Lord will rule over you."' Judg.
    8:22–3.
36 Zech. 4:11–14.

after he had deposed Abiathar, High Priest of the House of Aaron.[37]

In Jesus' day, the High Priesthood was held by those who called themselves Sadducees, or Zadokites, though they were not even authentically from the line of Melchizedek. The Epistle to the Hebrews envisions Jesus as the authentic Zadokite High Priest who does away with the 'johnny-come-lately' post-Hasmonean priests of the House of Caiaphas and Annas. Yet Hebrews does not address the original covenant with Aaron and his House in the wilderness tradition.

Luke provides the solution in the preliminaries of his Gospel:

> In the days of King Herod of Judea, there was a priest named Zechariah, who belonged to the [ancient levitical] priestly order of Abijah. His wife was a *descendant of Aaron*, and her name was Elizabeth.[38]

And the angel Gabriel said to Mary:

> Moreover, your *kinswoman* Elizabeth has also conceived a son in her old age; and this is now the sixth month for her who was called barren, for with God nothing will be impossible.[39]

As in many matrilineal societies, the lineage of the mother is at least equal to and often more important than that of the father. In Israel, the child follows the mother, and every son is adopted by the father on the eighth day of circumcision, when the child is made a member of the father's covenant with the God of Abraham.[40]

---

37 1 Kings 2:26f. Abiathar was deposed because he had not supported Solomon, Bath Sheba (Solomon's mother) and Nathan the prophet in stealing the kingship for Solomon from Solomon's older brother Adonijah, the rightful heir, in a palace coup.

38 Luke 1:5.

39 Luke 1:36–7.

40 In Roman tradition, a child was acknowledged by the father only when and if he picked it up from the ground. With regard to

We see, then, that God has indeed fulfilled in Jesus the
ancient covenant with Aaron, the authentic High Priest
from earliest times; he begins that ministry at the age of
thirty, the prescribed age for a Levite to undertake ministry.
He is baptized by his cousin, John the Baptist, and on that
occasion:

> And while he prayed, the heaven was opened and the Holy
> Spirit descended upon him in bodily form like a dove
> [Jonah]. And a voice came from heaven, 'You are my Son,
> the one that I love; in you I am well pleased'.[41]

Here, again in Luke's Gospel,[42] we see the High Priest
anointed by God with his own Spirit; and filled, then, with
that Spirit, Jesus undertakes the high priestly liturgy as the
Lamb of God.

How was it possible for the High Priest to give his life as
the sacrifice of the atonement and still live? It is important
to understand the principle of 'the laying on of hands', or
ordination. In the great iconic story of the sacrifice of the
Atonement, namely the sacrifice by Abraham of his son
Isaac in Genesis 22, Abraham is called upon to give back to
God that which God had provided, namely his inheriting
son Isaac. We recall that Abraham was ninety-nine years
and Sarah, his wife, was eighty-nine years old and barren
when Isaac was born. Clearly this was a God-provided
son, as it was impossible for the couple to have a child
otherwise.

As Abraham gets even older, it is important to God that
he have for his own the next generation of Abraham,

---

parentage and blood, the only sure parent is the mother; the father is
always unsure, and thus he must in some way 'adopt' the child. Jesus'
lineage in the House of David must be secondary to his lineage in the
House of Aaron – through his mother!

41 Luke 3:21–2.
42 Perhaps it is significant that the 'beast' symbol of Luke is the ox, the
symbol of the high priestly family.

namely Isaac, to remember his Name in the world. Thus he says: 'Give me your son, your only son, the one that you love [have designated your heir for the future] by sacrificing him on a mountain I will show you'.[43] Abraham departs immediately, taking with him the fire and the knife; he places the wood for the sacrifice on the back of Isaac his son, much as Jesus, too, carried the wood of his sacrifice on his back. As Abraham and Isaac are walking together, Isaac becomes suspicious: 'Papa, I see the fire and the knife; but where is the young lamb for the sacrifice, Papa?' Abraham's reply is filled with grief: 'God provides for himself the young lamb for the sacrifice – my son.' Now Isaac knows

---

43 Gen. 22:2f. There is a mistaken belief today that a sacrifice is about killing animals (or people) and that the more blood that is shed, the more effective the sacrifice. Thus a recent film about the crucifixion of Jesus is full of blood and gore as though this were the passion of Jesus. Such a misapprehension of sacrifice does not belong to the Bible at all. Biblical sacrifice is the offering to God of something with value to the offerer. To sacrifice, then, is to hand over completely the valued object and thus to be 'quit' of it. Because of the object's value to the offerer, the sacrifice is, in fact, an offering of the offerer's very life.

A second distinction must be made between the sacrifice and the means used to dispatch the offering. For an inanimate offering like grain or incense, the dispatch is achieved by burning (immolation) in some way. With liquid the means of dispatch is libation or pouring out. With living things, the means of dispatch is properly called slaughter. A distinction must be made, however, between sacrifice (binding or handing over) and slaughter (the means used to accomplish the handing over). The blood of living things as the bearer of the life itself adds a further complication. The slaughter of an animal for eating its meat requires that the blood (life) be returned to God, the author of life. This returning the blood (life) to God is not necessarily a sacrifice but the fulfilment of God's command that all life be returned to him. Sometimes the blood is sprinkled to bind a contract with the life-force; but this is not a sacrifice either.

In the case of Abraham and Isaac, God asks for the sacrifice of Isaac, the handing over of that which is of ultimate value to Abraham, for Isaac is Abraham's assurance of immortality. It is the slaughter of Isaac that God prevents, allowing the ram caught in the thicket to be used for the actual slaughter.

that he is the lamb of God which God himself has provided. Isaac assents to his own sacrifice (that is, he *suffers* himself to be the sacrifice), for the text continues: 'And the two of them walked on together'. He is willing and suffers this thing to happen.

God shows Abraham the place of sacrifice and Abraham builds an altar there, setting the wood and preparing the fire for the immolation. Then he 'binds' his son Isaac. The word 'bind' is only used here in the Old Testament and has the sense of 'binding over' or 'giving completely'; Abraham is quit of his son. As he raises the knife for the slaughter, the angel of God screams from heaven: 'Don't do it!'[44] Abraham looks up and sees a ram caught by its horns in the thicket nearby. Because it is caught by its horns rather than its wool, it is unblemished and a worthy victim.

Abraham takes the ram (lays hands on it) and sacrifices it in the stead of his son Isaac. This laying on hands extends the life of Abraham and Isaac to the ram – the ram actually becomes the reality of the life of Abraham and Isaac. Such an action is much more than a mere substitution – the lamb shares the actual life of the one who lays hands on it with purpose. The same principle holds true in the Catholic Church when the bishop lays his hands on an ordinand and extends his own life (spirit) to him, empowering the ordained priest with the bishop's own power and authority.[45]

44 An ancient rabbinic tradition from the time of Jesus says that Abraham began to argue with God: 'But you told me to do it! Why have you changed your mind? Maybe you are the Satan and not God at all.' The angel persists. Finally Abraham makes a bargain with God: 'I won't slaughter him if, in the future, when the children (descendants) of this boy sin, you will not look at their sins but remember what I did here.' God is said to have replied: 'OK, you're on.' The blowing of the ram's horn, the shofar, is the reminder to God of this promise.

45 We see the same principle at work in Numbers: The Lord said to Moses, 'Assemble seventy elders from Israel ... I will take back part of that same spirit which has been conferred on you and confer it on them, and they will share with you the burden of taking care for the

On the Day of Atonement, two identical beasts, male kids, are brought to the High Priest as he is dressed in his vestments with the crown of glory on his brow. He takes the sacred lots (*Urim* and *Thummim*) from the breastplate and casts them before the pair of animals to discern which is to be designated for Azazel, the demon of the wilderness – the so-called 'scapegoat' – and which of them is to be the lamb of God.

The High Priest holds his hands over the head of the 'scapegoat', makes confession over it and places the culpability or burden of the sins of Israel on the beast, which is then sent out into the wilderness, there to fall over the precipice and break its neck. A red cord had been tied to its horns and the other end to a rock, and when it falls over the cliff and dies, tradition has it that the red cord turns white from the bleaching of the sunlight, recalling the Psalm: 'Though your sins be as scarlet, they shall become whiter than snow'.

The exact formula of the High Priest in conveying the sins of Israel to the 'scapegoat' is unknown to us. Some scholars[46] have suggested that the sins of the people over the course of the preceding year came to rest upon the Temple itself or on some part of it (perhaps the *kapporeth*), being drawn to it like a magnet. Notice it is not the sin itself which is the problem but the guilt which arises from the sin,

---

people; then you will not have to bear it alone.' Numbers 11:16–17.

Similarly we see concerning the Levites in Numbers 8:10–11: 'Bring the Levites before the Lord, and let the Israelites lay their hands on their heads. Aaron shall present the Levites before the Lord as a special offering from the Israelites, and they shall be dedicated to the service of the Lord.'

46 An idea apparently first proposed by Julian Morgenstern in his *Doctrine of Sin in the Babylonian Religion* first published in 1905 through the University of Heidelberg and later developed in a plethora of articles in the *Hebrew Union College Annual*. For a fulsome discussion of Yom Kippur and the atonement sacrifice, see Shalom Adler-Rudel, 'Atonement' in *The Encyclopaedia Judaica*, Vol. 3, pp. 830f (Keter Publishing House, Ltd., Jerusalem, 1972).

which guilt has weight and is a burden which pollutes the dwelling of God and which must be regularly removed, lest God depart from his holy habitation. The High Priest wiped the pollution[47] from the Temple and transferred it to the 'scapegoat', thereby to be taken away to Azazel in the wilderness.[48]

However, there is no suggestion of any identification between the 'scapegoat' and the High Priest here. He does not place his hands on the animal and extend his life to it. The High Priest is here only the agent or instrument for the gathering and transferring of the pollution of sin. Nor is the 'scapegoat' to be considered a sacrifice in any way, for it is not slaughtered nor its blood shed. Rather, like Jesus bar Abbas in the Passion stories, it is allowed to go free bearing the pollutions; and like Judas Iscariot, it ends up committing suicide (both Judas and the 'scapegoat' are described as hanging themselves) away from the people. There is no consideration of the life blood or the body of the 'scapegoat'. The 'scapegoat' does not make expiation in any way between God and the people. In short, the 'scapegoat' is preliminary to the rite of Atonement, just as Moses first had to get rid of the pollution of the golden calf and the ensuing chaos of the people before he could return to God to restore the relationship between God and the people.

In reality, the casting of lots had as its real purpose to set aside the animal designated for God through which the

---

47 The Hebrew word for 'atonement' has some connection with 'wiping' or 'lifting off'.
48 We do know the prayer of the High Priest over the scapegoat in the time of the Second Temple from the *Mishnah*: 'I pray, O Eternal! Thy people, the house of Israel, have done wrong, they have transgressed, they have sinned before Thee. I pray, by Thy Name! Pardon, I pray, the iniquities, the transgressions, and the sins which Thy people, the house of Israel, have wrongly committed, and which they have transgressed, and which they have sinned before Thee, as it is written [Lev. 16:30] in the Law of Moses, Thy servant, "For on This day shall atonement be made for you to cleanse you from all your sins, before the Eternal shall ye be clean"' (*Mishnah*, Yoma 6:2).

High Priest could offer his life to reconcile the people with the Lord. What is most important for us in understanding the 'sign of Jonah' is that the atonement offering for the Lord is for the reconciliation of the people of Israel; it in no way touches upon the reconciliation of those outside the community of Israel – the Gentiles and the nations. For the Gentiles there was no sacrifice of atonement; there was no one to bear the responsibility for sin no matter how frightened they might be or how unwitting their offences against the Almighty. There was no High Priest for the Nations. But now in our parable of Jonah, the lot falls on Jonah – he knows who the sacrifice must be for these pagan sailors so that they will not die in the storm.

I. 8 *They said to him, 'Tell us why this calamity has come upon us. What is your occupation? From where have you come – what is your country and of what people are you?'*

Jonah is an unknown, a passenger rather than a crewman. The sailors know nothing about him save that the lot fell on him as being able to offer a remedy to their imminent death. Of course, they want to know all about him, his work, his part of the world and his nationality. We are meant to understand that Jonah is foreign to them, and in like manner, they are Gentiles to Jonah. Their questions here are only preliminary, however, to their real question in verse 11.

I. 9 *So he said to them, 'I am a Hebrew; and I fear the Lord, the God of heaven, who made the sea and the dry land'.*

Jonah identifies himself as a 'Hebrew' rather than specifically as an Israelite. To call oneself a Hebrew is to use a generalized identity, much like calling oneself an 'American' rather than saying 'I am from Peru'. The Israelites as a people were fairly insignificant from a global perspective.

Far more important to the sailors is the God whom Jonah
fears (worships). And far from being the God of one particular people, this God is the single God of heaven who made
everything that is. The God behind the storm is not the god
of a storm, or the god of the sea or of some aspect of the
land. This is the Creator-God of all of creation who made
everything.

Fear and worship or 'having faith in' are all the same
thing here, in the sense that the deity I fear is the one to
whom I have entrusted my life and all my hopes for life, and
in whom I have placed my faith even in the face of death.
The sailors have taken their lives in their own hands since
their gods cannot or will not help them. Therefore they are
in fear of their lives and of losing them; Jonah on the other
hand has put his faith in the God who has created everything, including life itself, and is therefore not afraid of the
death-dealing storm. Jonah's God has ultimate power over
the storm.

I. 10 *Now the men were even more terrified, and they said to him, 'Why have you done this?' The men knew that he had fled from the Lord's presence because he had told them.*

The terror of the sailors becomes even greater when they
hear of the power of the God behind the storm – not just a
deity, but the God, Creator of heaven and earth. They cannot
understand what Jonah has told them about his attempt to
get away from hearing the Word of the Lord so that he would
not have to proclaim it. They know nothing about the Lord,
and the mission laid upon Jonah to Nineveh would mean
little to them and any connection between Jonah's present
course of action and the storm is completely lost on them.
Nor is it important in our parable here.

'What have you done?' is the grave question with which
God confronts Cain in Genesis 4:10 after he has murdered
his brother Abel. The force of the question here is really,
'Do you know the meaning and the staggering conse-

quences of what you have done?' Perhaps the sailors' question to Jonah is really the Lord's question in the mouths of the unwitting crewmen: 'Jonah, do you know the consequences of your running away? The lives of these sailors are in your hands. Do something!'

How often does our insularity and self-absorption cause us to run from our God's will for the world? Caught in our own little concerns and convictions about what is 'fair' for others, we resort to the comfort of sleep and fail to see the larger picture of God the Creator's desire for his world. He shakes us awake with the voice of a terrified world and says, 'What in this hell are you doing? We're dying, and you don't care!'

I. 11 *'What shall we do with you,' they asked, 'to make the sea go down?' For the storm grew worse and worse.*

Having discovered that Jonah is 'it' in terms of being the only one aboard with any kind of understanding about the storm, they now ask the obvious but terrifying question, 'What do we do now – with you?' In a real sense Jonah has himself become for them the solution and they want to know how to deal with Jonah. Behind their question is their awakening to Jonah's God and that Jonah's God must have a liturgy to make their terror of death abate. The starkness of the question, 'What should we do with or to you, Jonah?' brings the 'sign of Jonah' into sharp relief. Again we are reminded of 'the jonah' as an atoning sacrifice for sins of uncleanness and false vows.

I. 12 *'Take me [bind me] and throw me into the sea; then the sea will become calm for you. For now I know that this great storm can be on my account [as in 'tab', 'tally' or 'bill'].'*

Jonah does not say simply, 'Throw me overboard' but 'Take me [seize me] and throw me overboard'. 'Take me' has the same force as God's order to Abraham, 'Take your son, your only son, the one that you love ...'. Jonah, like Isaac, is to become the extension of the sacrificer(s) through the laying on of hands. This is the real meaning of the 'binding' of Isaac; it is not tying up with cords but is used in the legal sense of 'binding over' or 'offering completely'. That Jonah is offering himself as a sacrifice according to the ancient formula of the High Priest on the Day of Atonement is clear. We are reminded of Moses' offer: 'If you will forgive them, then fine and good. But if you will not forgive them, take my life in the stead of theirs.' And God's reply to Moses, 'Rather, it is Aaron's life I will accept'. But here Jonah is offering himself for *Gentiles*!

If there were simply a need for Jonah to die, he would have jumped into the sea himself and committed suicide.[49] But here they must 'take him', lay their hands on him first, so that Jonah becomes the extension of their own lives and his life the means through which they offer their lives to the Lord God; and only then to slaughter him.[50] This 'taking him' may be seen in the Passion narratives of Jesus at each point from the Mount of Olives to the crucifixion.

Jesus could have committed suicide – perhaps jumped from the pinnacle of the Temple as the Satan tempted him to do – if all that was important was that he die. Rather he went to elaborate planning to set up his sacrifice. To initiate the process of 'binding over', he tells his disciples that one of them would have to initiate the liturgy. 'Does it have to be me?' they all cry out. 'The one who has his hand in the dish with me now is "it" – the one who must bind me over[51]

---

49 In the *Mekilta* cited above, 'R. Nathan says: "Jonah made his voyage only in order to drown himself in the sea, for thus it is said: 'And he said unto them: Take me up and cast me forth into the sea.' (Jonah 1.12)". R. Nathan does not see the importance of Jonah's action as sacrifice.'

50 In Scripture, 'slaughter' is to take life with the permission of the life-Giver; 'murder' is to take life without the permission of the life-Giver. 'Killing' is a generic and not a specific enough word.

51 The Greek word usually translated 'betray' may also be used in this technical sacrificial sense of 'binding over' as in the story of the

on behalf of the company of the disciples and initiate the liturgy of the atonement.' He is then bound over to the Temple guard on the Mount of Olives (though Peter does not understand this free-will offering on Jesus' part and draws his sword). They in turn bind him over to the High Priest who has already used the high priestly formula concerning Jesus:

> Now many of the Judeans who had come to visit Mary and had seen what Jesus did [with the raising of Lazarus], put their faith in him. But some of them went off to the Pharisees and reported what he had done. Thereupon the chief priests and the Pharisees convened a meeting of the Sanhedrin. 'What action are we going to take?' they said. 'This man is performing many signs. If we leave him alone like this the entire populace will believe in him. Then the Romans will come and sweep away our Temple and our nation.' But one of them, Caiaphas, who was High Priest that year, said, 'You know nothing whatever; you do not use your judgement; it is more to your interest that one man should die for the people, than that the whole nation should be destroyed.' He did not say this of his own accord, but as the High Priest that year, he was prophesying that Jesus should die for the nation – should die not for the nation alone but to gather together the scattered children of God. So from that moment they planned his death.[52]

The High Priest then binds Jesus over to the Gentile authority, Pontius Pilate the Procurator and the legate of the Emperor Tiberius himself. In Luke's Gospel, Pilate binds Jesus over to the foreign-born (Idumean = Edomite) princeling of Galilee, Herod Antipas, whose curiosity about Jesus was met with Jesus' silence. Herod's court then

---

'Binding' of Isaac. Paul uses this same word in speaking of the Passion. For scholars, the word is $\pi\alpha\rho\alpha\delta\acute{\iota}\delta\omega\mu\iota$ = עקד.

52 John 11:45–54.

mocked Jesus, dressed him in 'gorgeous robes'[53] and bound him back to Pilate.[54] Pilate, after three times declaring Jesus' innocence, now stands Jesus before the people. Frustrated by the continuing cries for his crucifixion, he releases Jesus bar Abbas (rather like the scapegoat) and hands Jesus to the crowd to be crucified.

Matthew observes that at this point, Pilate washes his hands of the blood of Jesus (that is, his life). In so doing, he declares that he is not guilty of murder of an innocent but caught up in a liturgy that is much greater than even the Rome that he represents. The response of the crowd is noteworthy: 'His blood be upon us and upon our children forever'. This is not the blood of murder, for murder would suggest that they took Jesus' life from him, whereas in fact Jesus quite clearly offers his life freely. What is freely offered cannot be stolen! In fact, it appears from the

53 Here and elsewhere there are intimations of the vestments of the High Priest, especially the seamless robe. See below. For a thrilling picture of the High Priest's splendid vestments on the Day of Atonement, read: 'How splendid he was with the people thronging round him, when he emerged from the curtained shrine, like the morning star among the clouds, like the moon at the full, like the sun shining on the Temple of the Most High, like the rainbow gleaming against brilliant clouds, like a rose in springtime, like a lily by a spring, like a branch of the incense tree in summer, like fire and incense in the censer, like a massive golden vessel encrusted with every kind of precious stone, like an olive tree loaded with fruit, like a cypress soaring to the clouds; when he took his ceremonial robe and put on his magnificent ornaments, when he went up to the holy altar and filled the sanctuary precincts with his grandeur; when he received the portions from the hands of the priests, himself standing by the altar hearth, crowned with the circle of his brothers, as a cedar of Lebanon is by its foliage, as though surrounded by the trunks of palm trees. When all the sons of Aaron in their glory, with the offerings of the Lord in their hands, stood before the whole assembly of Israel, while he completed the rites at the altars, nobly presenting the offerings to the Almighty, Most High!' Sirach 50:5–14.

54 Luke (23:12) adds that this movement of Jesus between Pilate, Herod and back again brought about a reconciliation between Herod and Pilate, who until this time had been enemies. The effect of the sacrificial victim brings peace even among Gentiles.

Passion narratives that Jesus has set up the entire liturgy of
the Passion. Rather, we are reminded here of the narrative
in Exodus:

> Moses took half the blood and put it in basins and the other
> half he flung against the altar. Then he took the Book of the
> Covenant and read it aloud for all the people to hear. They
> said, 'We will obey, and do all that the Lord has said.'
> Moses then took the blood and flung it over the people,
> saying, 'This is the blood of the covenant which the Lord
> has made with you on the terms of this book'.[55]

And again in the Book of the Chronicles:

> So the bulls were slaughtered, and the priests took their
> blood and flung it against the altar; the rams were slaugh-
> tered, and their blood was flung against the altar; the lambs
> were slaughtered, and their blood was flung against the
> altar. Then the he-goats for the atonement offering were
> brought before the king [Hezekiah] and the assembly, who
> laid their hands on them; and the priests slaughtered them
> and used their blood as a sin-offering on the altar to make
> atonement for all Israel. For the king had commanded that
> the whole-offering and the sin-offering should be made for
> all Israel.[56]

The chances are that Matthew, when he remembers the cry
of the people about Jesus, is recollecting these parts of the
tradition rather than setting up the Judeans as 'murderers'.

Pilate then hands or binds Jesus over to the soldiers who,
like the sailors on Jonah's ship, are men from every nation
under heaven. They begin, unknowingly, to vest Jesus in the
high priestly garments – the violet mantle which is a seamless robe: 'Make the mantle of the ephod a single piece of
violet stuff. There shall be a hole for the head in the middle

---

55 Ex. 24:6–8.
56 2 Chron. 29:22–4. The Chronicles were read together with Job by the
   High Priest, barefoot and standing on the Gabatha, on the night
   before the Atonement sacrifice.

of it'.[57] They fashioned also a crown of thorns, reminiscent of the crown of the High Priest:

> Set the crown [turban-mitre] on his head, and the symbol of holy dedication [with the Name of God engraved on it – 'Holy to the Lord'] on the crown. Take the anointing oil, pour it on his head and anoint him [Messiah]. Then bring his sons forward, invest them with tunics, gird them with the sashes and tie their tall head-dresses on them. They shall hold the priesthood by a covenant binding for all time.[58]

The soldiers also place a cane or reed in Jesus' right hand with which they beat him. Here we are reminded of Cain, the murderous brother of the innocent Abel, whose name means 'a reed or cane' and also 'jealousy' and 'anger' and through whom murder was first introduced into creation. Cain's great sin was the first forgiven by God, and the recollection here is surely a fine touch.

Jesus is then assisted with his cross by another foreigner, one Simon from Cyrene. He is taken to Golgotha, the place of rolling, and here we are reminded of the crossing of Israel of the Jordan River into the Promised Land under Joshua and the twelve Levites carrying the Ark.

> On the tenth day of the first month the people came up out of the Jordan and camped in Gilgal in the district east of Jericho, and there Joshua set up twelve stones which they had taken from the Jordan.
> When the circumcision of the whole nation was finished, they stayed where they were in camp until they had recovered [from the tenth day until the eve of Passover]. The Lord then said to Joshua, 'Today I have rolled back the sins of Egypt'. Therefore the place is called Gilgal[59] to this very day.[60]

---

57 Exod. 28:31. It is noteworthy that in Jesus' day the High Priest's vestments were held by the Romans in the Antonia Fortress next to the Temple, so that the High Priest could only make this most crucial sacrifice with the co-operation of the Procurator.

58 Exod. 29:6–9.

59 Gilgal is the place of rolling stones, or a stone circle – much like Stonehenge. The Aramaic for Gilgal is something very akin to Golgotha.

60 Joshua 4:19–20; 5:8–9.

Jesus is then bound to the wood of the cross just as Isaac is bound to the wood of the sacrifice in Genesis 22. Over Jesus' head is fixed the inscription: 'Jesus the Nazarene and the King of the Jews'.[61]

I. 13 *Nevertheless the men rowed hard to return to the dry land, but they could not, for the sea continued to grow more tempestuous against them.*

The interplay of the raging sea and the dry land is a reminder of the interplay of the chaos of the waters before the creation and the emergence of the dry land at the Word of God. We are also invited to recall the stormy waters of the Red Sea and the dry land of deliverance on the opposite shore. Likewise, in the parable of the crossing of the Jordan mentioned above, we have the raging flood of the river but the Children of Israel passing through on dry land. The salvation offered by the dry land is the goal of those caught in the dread of the raging storm.

The sailors are still trying to help themselves, putting their faith in their own seamanship and strength. This can only lead to increased terror. It is sometimes difficult to give up control to the Lord when we are used to and even proud of our self-reliance.

I. 14 *Only then did they cry out to the Lord and said, 'We pray, O Lord, please do not let us perish on the account of this man's life; and do not charge us with murder [of an innocent]; for all of this is your set purpose.'*

And now we come to the heart of the matter. The Gentile sailors, in their dread of impending death, call out to the

---

61 Perhaps it is not too fanciful that a possible Hebrew translation of the title היהודים והמלך הנזר ישוע using the first letter of each word spells *yod heh vav heh* (in Hebrew), YHWH the Holy Name of God which was also on the brow of the High Priest on the crown. It would be small wonder, then, that the priests objected so violently to this sign above Jesus' head on the cross.

Lord God of Israel. They know of him only because Jonah has finally told them where lies their salvation. They accept the principle 'the sacrifice of the one who is innocent to save the lives of the many' ("take my life in the stead of theirs"). 'Father, forgive them for they did not know what they were doing.' To them it looks like murder, for they do not know the liturgy of the Day of Atonement; yet they plead with the Almighty that it not be attributed to them as murder – the sin of sins – on the grounds that the liturgy outlined to them by Jonah is clearly God's own liturgy. They do not understand it, but are willing to do it to save their lives.

Clearly Jonah is considered an innocent; his attempted escape from a prophetic ministry is certainly not a sin and is between himself and God, not affecting the sailors nor depriving Jonah of his suitability as the sacrificial means of their atonement and thus their salvation.

One of the most powerful lines in the entire Bible, 'All of this is your set purpose [liturgy], O Lord' is perhaps the underlying principle of all Scripture, from the Liturgy of Creation to the Liturgy of the New Heaven and Earth. It is God's doing, not ours. It is the perfect declaration of faith: 'Not my will, but yours be done'.

It should be apparent that 'liturgy' and 'parable' as defined in chapter one are fairly interchangeable concepts so far as the Bible is concerned. For example, that parable of the prodigal son is actually my story which is verifiable in my time, place and experience. The liturgy of the prodigal son is the action of alienation, dissolution with sinful behaviour, repentance and restoration, without the narrative. So here in the parable of Jonah; we have the narrative of Jonah's offering of his life for the sailors as well as the liturgy of the 'binding of the victim' for the atonement. Every liturgy can be expanded into a narrative; the praxis of every narrative can be reduced to the liturgy of it. 'Liturgy' and 'parable' are the Bible's only real 'theology'.

I. 15 *So they seized Jonah and threw him into the sea; and the sea ceased from its raging.*

It is finished; *missa est*; the liturgy is completed according to the rite established by God. Around the cross, the storm raged and the creation was disintegrating. Then Jesus offered his life – he finished the Liturgy. There is no hope for personal reward; the sacrifice is a pure self-offering: 'My God, my God, why have you forsaken me?' Finally he binds over his own life: 'Into your hands, O Lord, I commit my spirit'. The storm resolves into peace. The Gentile centurion and his cohort at the foot of the cross reach out and, like the sailors on Jonah's ship, declare their faith: 'Truly, this man is the son of God'.

I. 16 *The men feared the Lord greatly; they made a sacrifice to the Lord and they made vows [of their faith in the Lord].*

It is interesting to note that this first part of the parable ends with the results for the sailors. Jonah and his situation are not mentioned at all. Rather we hear of the conversion of the sailors and their salvation, which is the real point of the narrative. We know they are converted in that they substitute their fear of death with the fear of the Lord. Their self-reliance and the pride in themselves have been defeated by the storm and reduced them to the fear of death. Now they rely on the Lord and their fear of the Lord (faith) is 'great'. They make offerings to the Lord and declare their faith in him with unswerving vows. 'Do not be afraid,' says Jesus, 'it is I; and I have overcome the world' – and its fear and death.

The 'sign of Jonah' is a sign of God's desire to save the Gentiles, that is, humankind awash in the terror of a world which sin is destroying. For God so loved the world that he gave over his Son, his only Son, the one that he loved, so that all that believe in him, who lay their hands on the sacrifice, will not die, but have life eternal. Furthermore, Jonah becomes the High Priest for the Gentile sailors who have no other hope for life. He is the Suffering (willing) Servant (of God), the remnant of Israel spared from the Assyrian conquest to call Assyria to repentance and salvation. Jonah becomes the willing sacrifice, suffering the sacrifice of his life for Gentiles; Jesus, the son of Adam, gives us the same sign.

I. 17 (II.1 *in some versions*) *Now the Lord had prepared a great fish to swallow up Jonah. And Jonah was in the belly of the fish for three days and three nights.*

And now we come, finally, to the fish – the great sea monster. Far from being the 'whale' of my Sunday School teacher's researches, however, this monster transcends anything in the normal order of creation and is undoubtedly the 'leviathan' of ancient Near Eastern tradition, the monster which represents the chaos itself. He is the monster of the sea as 'behemoth' is the monster of the land and 'ziz' the monster of the air.

Clearly 'leviathan' is the chaos of death itself, the great dragon or ramping serpent who is the enemy to the orderliness of life. Yet this is not death as we understand it, that is, the cessation of physical functioning of the individual in this world; rather it is the death which is exile. We must remember that 'life' in pre-Exilic Israel is defined as the continuity of the family name (the patrimony) on its designated plot of land (in a sense, its matrimony, as land always passes through the mother's line) from generation to generation. The eldest son in each generation is the promise of eternal life, and the land – which can never be sold outright – is the continuing source of food and drink (bread and wine) for each and every generation. Through the generations, each eldest son must remember those who have gone before on a family 'Day', which causes them to stay alive 'in their place'.[62] This perpetual remembrance of

---

62 This annual 'Day' of the revitalization of the family is perhaps what David uses as his excuse for not attending upon King Saul, when he

the ancestors is the true meaning of the commandment 'Honour your father and your mother'; that is, keeping them alive by naming them regularly on the family land.[63]

Of course, it is God who gives the children and God who gives and guarantees the land. Or to say it another way, it is God who gives life. When God promises Abraham eternal life, he does so by guaranteeing him offspring 'like the stars of the sky and sands of the sea for number' and offers him 'a land in which to dwell in perpetuity'.[64] Abraham in return must have God as his God in perpetuity, as signed by the covenant of the circumcision of all male children. Here is a covenant of Life Everlasting.

When the Israelites enter the Promised Land, God again gives each tribal family its appointed portion of the land – except his special servants, the Levites, who are to have no land to sustain their families, as God guarantees their sustenance through tithes of the people and makes the Levites his own family. While they do have children, the Levites are nonetheless celibate in that they have no land and cannot make 'a living' for themselves. Their eternal life is different from the rest in that they do not participate in obtaining it. Theirs is to be a model of faith and dependence upon God for their future, and it is a real risk.[65]

Given this understanding concerning eternal life, it is no wonder that exile, which means alienation from God's land

---

asks Jonathan to tell Saul: 'David asked me for leave to pay a rapid visit to his home in Bethlehem, for it is the annual sacrifice there for the whole family'. (I Samuel 20:6)

63 So in Ruth 4:10 (once more in Bethlehem), Boaz' intention of taking Ruth as another wife is 'to perpetuate the name of the deceased (Mahlon, and by extension Mahlon's entire family) with his patrimony, so that his name may not go missing among his kindred and at the gate of his native place (his land)'. So critical is this eldest son that the Bible can even (though barely) condone incest, as in the case of Lot and his daughters (Gen. 19:33–7), and incest/prostitution in the case of Judah and his daughter-in-law Tamar. (Gen. 38:12–27)

64 Gen. 17:1–8, for example.

65 Here are to be found the real origins of celibacy for the priesthood in the Roman Catholic Church.

and the break-up of families, is equated to profound death
and annihilation far beyond the physical death of any individual. Exile is oblivion of all the generations preceding and
is catastrophic rather than simply uncomfortable. So the
experiences of Israel's exile, whether in Egypt, in Assyria or
in Babylon become 'leviathan'; they are both Sheol and the
chaos which is hell.

We meet 'leviathan' several times in the great parable of
Job; in Isaiah 'leviathan' is the monster of the overthrow
of Jerusalem whom God will overthrow at the time of
restoration:

> That day, the Lord will punish,
> with His hard sword, massive and strong,
> Leviathan the fleeing serpent,
> Leviathan the twisting serpent:
> He will kill the sea-dragon.[66]

The origin of this 'leviathan', the twisting dragon, may well
be the experience of Israel in Egypt, the hell on earth and
the prototype of exile. The twisting dragon is probably the
Nile, the great monster of Egypt, which has enormous
power to hold peoples in thrall. So we see later on in Isaiah:

> Awake, awake! Clothe yourself in strength,
> arm of the Lord.
> Awake, as in the past,
> in times of generations long ago.
> Did you not split Rahab in two,
> and pierce the dragon through?
> Did you not dry up the sea,
> the waters of the great Abyss,
> to make the seabed a road
> for the redeemed to cross?[67]

The reference to the crossing of the Red Sea is evident, the

66 Isa. 27:1.
67 Isa. 51:9–10.

coming out of the hell which is Egypt and being born again as the people of God, as they pass through the waters which the Lord has split. Isaiah views the new redemption in the terms of the first one.

> I am the Lord your God who stirs the sea, making its waves roar, my name is the Lord Sabaoth. I put My words in your mouth, I hid you in the shadow of My hand, when I planted the heavens and laid the earth's foundations and said to Zion, 'You are my people'.[68]

Furthermore, the emergence from 'leviathan', from the chaos of Egypt, is clearly seen in terms of resurrection:

> Your dead will come to life,
> their corpses will rise;
> awake and exult,
> all you who live in the dust,
> for your dew is a radiant dew
> and the land of ghosts (Sheol) will give birth.[69]

But it must be made clear that biblical resurrection is not to be defined by our particular obsession with personal existence in the afterlife, which was ever the concern of the nobility of Egypt and especially of the Pharaohs. Scripture's resurrection is a community (family) one, and St Paul makes it clear that the resurrection of Jesus is only the 'first-fruits of those who sleep [in the family of Jesus, the Church]'.[70]

Jonah's sojourn in the belly of the fish is to last three days. Since the three-day journey into the tomb which Jesus anticipates for himself is surely related to the experience of Jonah, we might well wonder why it is to be three days. The answer is speculative but based on some scriptural evidence.

We have already referred to the parable of the Binding of

68 Isa. 51:14–16.
69 Isa. 26:19.
70 I Cor. 15:20–3.

Isaac in Genesis 22 as the iconic narrative for the Day of Atonement. In Genesis 22:4 we read: 'On the third day Abraham lifted up his eyes and saw the place afar off'. The liturgy of the great sacrifice would seem to be a seven-day feast. Three days are the days of 'going out' to the place designated by God. Then there is the middle or fourth day for the sacrifice itself. Finally there are the three days of returning. With regard to the great Pilgrim Festivals of later Israel, an eighth day was added for recovery and rest from the journey. This is perhaps the origin of what the Catholic Church celebrates as octaves for the major feasts.

Another hint is to be found in the story of Joseph in Egypt. Joseph's arrogance in the use of his gifts has caused a threefold 'fall' into hell. First his brothers throw him into the dry well; next he descends into the hell that is Egypt; and finally he is thrown into the dungeon for his dalliance with the wife of Potiphar. While in the dungeon he meets the two servants of Pharaoh, the butler or wine-bearer of Pharaoh and Pharaoh's baker.

While it is tempting to make something of the bread and the wine here, perhaps the bread of affliction and the cup of salvation, we must shun the temptation and turn rather to the theme of three. Both these servants of Pharaoh have dreams and discover that Joseph can interpret them. Both dreams are similar with regard to 'three days' and 'lifting or raising up.' Joseph's interpretation is as follows:

> Then Joseph said to him [the butler], 'This is its interpretation: the three branches are three days; after three days Pharaoh will lift up your head and restore you to your office; and you shall place Pharaoh's cup in his hand as formerly, when you were his butler.'
>
> And Joseph answered [the baker], 'This is its interpretation: the three baskets are three days; after three days Pharaoh will lift up your head – from you! – and hang you on a tree; and the birds will eat the flesh from you.'[71]

---

71 Gen. 40:12–13;18–19.

This same theme of the three days and raising up is reiterated in the parable of the coming out from Egypt. In Exodus 8:27 Moses tells Pharaoh: 'We must go three days' journey into the wilderness and sacrifice to the Lord our God as he will command us'. And further along we read that Moses led the people of Israel out of their homes in Egypt at the Feast of Passover and brought them to the shores of the Red Sea on the third day. The wonder and great sign of their coming up out of the waters of the Sea happened on the next day, the fourth day, and is in a real sense the coming back to life of Israel after the exile/hell of Egypt. In like manner, the Christian Day of Resurrection follows the three days of Jesus in the tomb.

Israel's passing through the Jordan at the end of their forty-year wanderings in the wilderness is a duplicate of the parable of the crossing of the Red Sea. Thus we are not surprised when we read:

> [And Joshua said,] 'Pass through the camp, and command the people: "Prepare your provisions; for in three days you are to cross over the Jordan, to go in to take possession of the land that the Lord your God gives you to possess."'[72]

Nor is it surprising that when Israel arrives in the Promised Land on the fourth day, they keep the Passover for the first time since they left Mount Sinai. For Christians, the transits through the waters, both through the sea which delivers them to the safety of the wilderness and through the waters of the Jordan which delivers them into God's land of promise, are of equal weight in understanding the Paschal Feast.

Finally, we have an evidence of the 3 + 1 + 3 sequence of the feasts in later tradition:

> And all the feasts and sabbaths and new moons and appointed days, and the three days before a feast and the

72 Josh. 1:11.

three after a feast — let them all be days of immunity and release for all the Jews who are in my kingdom.[73]

While there is nothing definite about this understanding of three days, perhaps we may at least make the observation that the coming out or rising up from the waters follows three days in the grave.

73 1 Macc. 10:34.

Chapter Two

The Exile, both of Israel in Assyria, and of Jerusalem and Judah in Babylon, accounts for much of the Bible's writings. To understand more fully chapter two of Jonah we must first reflect on the effects of the Exile on the people of God. We may perhaps discern stages of Israel's response to the catastrophe which was the Exile.

The generations before the Exile of Israel and in Jerusalem before the Exile of Judah had been living what to them was a normal life. They were more or less faithful to their God and probably no less or more faithful in the worship of the Lord and in carrying out his precepts and laws in their daily living. In this way they were probably no different from ourselves, neither very bad nor exceptionally virtuous. Life went on and seemed normal just as our life and the life of our nations we interpret as 'normal'.

The threat of the rise of foreign powers, Assyria and Babylonia, was probably vague for a long time, just as Egypt had been a perpetual problem and sometimes an affliction. Yes, the prophets did speak to moral decay and used the threat of the intervention of God to bring an end to immorality by withdrawing his support for his people; but for the most part the threat was not immediate and thus not particularly forceful or even meaningful. Again, they

were like us. We have our prophets who speak in the name
of the Lord against immorality and societal decay. Yet we,
too, often miss the big picture in the details of daily life and
presume there will never be a reckoning. Nor do we see
great political and social events as in some way involving
God as well as ourselves.

The destruction of Israel by Assyria, and of Judah and
Jerusalem by Babylon, come as a surprise and a shock to the
people. Their first response is, as ours would be, incredulity
that their God, the God of their fathers, the God who gave
them the land and sustained their nations, could possibly
allow the disaster to happen. And the initial reaction to
overthrow and Exile is simply the pain and rawness of it! It
does not make sense and yet it has happened, the deaths and
slaughter, the destruction of land and cities, the tearing
down of temples and holy places. This first reaction is a
sense of the pit, of Sheol and hell – of the end of all things.
There is naught to do at first but to stand in the wilderness
amid the destruction and wail.

Worse, perhaps, for a people whose glory had been their
God and who had been his favourites, the tearing down of
the temples and holy places suggested abandonment by the
Lord their God and their Defender. As the only God and the
creator of heaven and earth, the Lord had revealed himself
as the origin of all that happens; there was no possibility in
Israel's theology that 'gods' of other nations were responsible for the catastrophe.[1] Yet how was it possible for the
God who had made covenants with his people to forsake
them now and allow them to fall into the hands of the
enemy – or perhaps, horror of horrors, even deliver them

1 That Israel, from very earliest time, attributed everything, no matter
  how painful, to God is indicated by Naomi's response to the people
  of Bethlehem when she returns from Moab: 'I went away full, but the
  Lord has brought me back empty; why call me Naomi when the Lord
  has dealt harshly with me, and the Almighty has brought calamity
  upon me?' Ruth 1:21. This is not 'misfortune'; rather it is God's
  doing that Naomi should rename herself 'Mary' (*Mara* = 'bitterness')
  of Bethlehem.

into the hands of their foes? 'My God, my God; why have you forsaken me?'

The taunts of Israel's neighbours and their rejoicing over Israel's downfall and the apparent downfall of Israel's God, especially considering Israel's pride in the favouritism seemingly shown them by their God and their aloofness from the gods of others, only makes matters worse. National humiliation makes the sting and deadliness of Exile even worse.

After the pain has subsided and the shock of abandonment by God has dulled in Exile, the next stage is one of reflection: If God is never capricious and is always just, could the problem have been with Israel? Could the prophets have been right – the Exile is the consequence of Israel's sin and moral turpitude, a pollution of both people and the land itself which caused the expulsion of the nation? Certainly there is some estimation in the Bible of the Exile as a punishment.

This realization of sin, however, complicated matters further. The appointed method for dealing with sin had been the High Priest's liturgy on the Day of Atonement. Clearly that liturgy had not worked to avoid the Exile in the past, and now there was no longer a Temple, an altar, or a High Priest for the liturgy. Nor could there be such a liturgy on foreign territory, as it was understood that God did not act or speak in foreign lands. Thus we find long prayers of penitence, confession and spiritual mortification as a substitute for the Atonement in the Exile. Amendment of life and cries for mercy become the norm.

Another stream of exilic thought raises the question of a possible meaning for God's action in the Exile beyond that of simple punishment. It springs from the wonder of why God spared a remnant of his people in Exile. It also arises from a sense of the injustice and unfairness of God in dealing with his people so harshly – 'Why did this happen to us; it's not fair!' The Book of Job is the parable of this stream of thought. The taunts of Job's three friends, couched in the trappings of consolation, raise the question: 'What did you do wrong, Job? You must have done something, because the rule is that the good are rewarded and the bad punished; you are being punished, therefore you must be bad.' Job's retort: 'I am innocent; yet God is punishing me' comes dangerously close to declaring God to be an unjust and hence capricious judge. Yet the parable of Job ends with a new idea:

> [The Lord says to Job's three friends], 'So now find seven bullocks and seven rams, and take them back with you to my servant Job and make a burnt offering for yourselves, while Job, my servant, offers prayers for you. I shall show him favour and shall not inflict my displeasure on you for not having spoken about me correctly, as my servant Job has done'.[2]

Astonishingly, God says that he will reward Job for all his suffering by saving Job's three friends, who like the Wise Men from the East[3] in Matthew's birth narrative represent the nations of the world – the Gentiles. The suggestion is that God's justice and his actions transcend any individual's sense of what is fair for self – God's justice has to do with the restoration of his entire creation and not the 'election' of any single people.

We are told that when God confronts Job out of the whirlwind at the end of Job's lamentations, he does so by asking Job if he sees the big picture of creation – a kind of 'Where were you, Job, when I created the heavens and the earth? Can you do it, and if not, don't speak to me about what is "fair"!' Then Job falls down and repents 'in dust

---

2 Job 42:8.
3 There was a tradition of wise men in the kingdom of Edom, across the Jordan from Israel to the east. The 'Three Wise Men' visiting Solomon, who sit with Job and who call on Jesus at his birth are probably from this same Edomite tradition. Samuel Sandmel, *The Hebrew Scriptures* (Alfred A. Knopf, New York, 1963) has proposed that the kingdom of Edom led a coalition of seven nations against Jerusalem in 485 BCE and destroyed the Second Temple of Zerubabel. Thus the temple of Jesus' day was the Third Temple beautified by Herod.

and ashes', not of his sins, but of his presumption in judging events as though he were God. Only then does God address him again as 'My servant Job'.

It is clear from this parable of Job that Israel's election is tied to Israel's mission in the world. When Israel interprets their election as some sort of favouritism to be presumed and taken for granted, God must put them back on track. The Exile is thus God's way of waking them from their self-satisfied slumber and moving them into the mission fields of the nations.[4]

As time goes on, the despair of Exile begins to yield glimmers of hope for restoration, so that Jerusalem might again be restored, this time to become the mountain of the Lord in the midst of the whole earth from which God's Word goes forth to all nations and to which all nations are drawn to come up and worship God. This restoration is framed as a resurrection of the moribund people of God, raised up to a new covenant, the terms of which will be written, not on tablets of stone, but on their hearts and in their minds. This resurrection is a re-enabling and revitalizing of God's people for the responsibilities of mission – to become 'a light to the nations'.

A lovely statement of this revitalization of the people of Israel which follows the very creation of Adam in the beginning is found in the book of the prophet Ezekiel:

> The hand of the Lord came upon me, and he brought me out by the spirit of the Lord and set me down in the middle of a valley; it was full of bones. He led me all around them; there were very many lying in the valley, and they were very dry. He said to me, 'Mortal, can these bones live?' I answered, 'O Lord God, you know.' Then he said to me, 'Prophesy to these bones, and say to them: O dry bones, hear the word of the Lord. Thus says the Lord God to these bones: I will cause breath to enter you, and you shall live. I will lay sinews on you, and will cause flesh to come upon you, and cover you with skin, and put breath in you, and you shall

4 Isa. 49:6.

live; and you shall know that I am the Lord.' So I prophesied as I had been commanded; and as I prophesied,
suddenly there was a noise, a rattling, and the bones came
together, bone to its bone. I looked, and there were sinews
on them, and flesh had come upon them, and skin had
covered them; but there was no breath in them. Then he said
to me, 'Prophesy to the breath, prophesy, mortal, and say to
the breath: Thus says the Lord God: Come from the four
winds, O breath, and breathe upon these slain, that they
may live.' I prophesied as he commanded me, and the breath
came into them, and they lived, and stood on their feet, a
vast multitude. Then he said to me, 'Mortal, these bones are
the whole house of Israel. They say, "Our bones are dried
up, and our hope is lost; we are cut off completely." Therefore prophesy, and say to them, Thus says the Lord God: I
am going to open your graves, and bring you up from your
graves, O my people; and I will bring you back to the land
of Israel. And you shall know that I am the Lord, when I
open your graves, and bring you up from your graves, O my
people. I will put my spirit within you, and you shall live,
and I will place you on your own soil; then you shall know
that I, the Lord, have spoken and will act, says the Lord.'[5]

We find here the threefold structure of Adam in the process
of the restoration of Israel. First the bones must come
together and be tied by sinews, constituting the body structure. The physical body is that which is most visible and by
which we know ourselves and each other. So it is with the
body of the people of Israel here. Yet the body by itself is
only an inanimate statue. There must also be a spirit, which
is the entirety of what is real about us but cannot be seen:
our thoughts, our feelings; our hopes and aspirations; our
understanding of ourselves and of the world and our place
in it. So too with the people of Israel; God's spirit or breath
is called up to animate the body.

Finally there is our name – our identity – which is always
given by the author of our life. In Hebrew, the 'name' is
comparable to what we call the 'soul', that which is most

5 Ezekiel 37:1–15.

profoundly us and is most unknown unless revealed. Our name suggests our purpose and *raison d'être*. It connects us with our progenitor and our progenitor's purpose in the world. Israel is (once again) in this passage from Ezekiel named 'My People' by their God, just as he had named them 'Not My People' or 'No One' before their Exile because they had departed from the plan and purpose of their Father: 'Then the Lord said, "Name him *Lo-ammi*, for you are not my people and I am not your God."'[6]

And what is the purpose of their Father for which Israel is created and now re-created? The Lord's ultimate purpose for his creation and humankind's place in it is best and most clearly stated by the prophet Zechariah, as he anticipates Israel's return from Exile:

> On that day living waters shall flow out from Jerusalem, half of them to the eastern sea and half of them to the western sea; it shall continue in summer as in winter. And the Lord will become king over all the earth; on that day the Lord will be one and his name one.[7]

The restoration of the kingdom of God, not the restoration or the advancement of any chosen people, is God's goal. 'Chosenness' of any individual or nation is chosenness to

---

6 Hos. 1:9. The Catholic Church in her Sacrament of Baptism uses this same understanding of the creation of Adam. The body comes out of the waters of the womb; the new body with Christ's body attached comes out of the womb of the Church, the font. The spirit is signified by oil, which is invisible yet real, just like the human spirit. The human spirit is given the spirit of Christ with the chrism. To the human name is attached the name of Christ, 'Christian' at the door of the Church. While Christ's body died on the cross, while his spirit was given up on the cross ('he breathed his last'), and while his name on the *titulus* died away with him, nonetheless God raised him, body, spirit and name on the third day. All those who bear his body ('Put on Christ'), spirit ('Receive the Holy Spirit') and name ('the Name that is above all other names') with him in baptism, even though they die, will live forever with him in their own resurrection. For his resurrection is the earnest of our own.

7 Zech. 14:8–9.

assist in achieving that goal. Chosenness is for service and mission and not most favoured status. The chosen servant of God is to be even self-sacrificial in order to get God's world back for him. There is a little passage tucked away in the Book of Sirach which suggests this purpose of suffering:

> Lift up your hand against foreign nations and let them see your might. Our sufferings proved your holiness to them, so use them to show your glory to us. Then they will know, as we have known that there is no God but you, O Lord.[8]

Thus Israel and Judah become the servants of God through whose sufferings the nations are saved. Here is the origin, of course, of the Suffering Servant of God summarized in the person of Job. And because Israel suffers or allows its life to be sacrificed for the nations, Israel becomes a kind of High Priest for the Nations just as is the case, as we have seen, with Jonah.[9]

Jesus undoubtedly anticipates a new Exile of Jerusalem and Judah with a pending destruction of Jerusalem by the Romans. This anticipation is the burden of Jesus' apocalyptic observations in the Gospels before his Passion. Therefore he offers the sign of Jonah as the interpretation of both his ministry and his pending sacrifice.

The Psalm of Jonah in chapter two is a kind of summary of the whole experience of Exile and its purpose. It informs the parable in chapter one which is mirrored in chapters three and four after Jonah's resurrection.

---

8 Sirach 36:3–5.
9 In a lovely passage in the prophet Hosea, we find God's relationship with his servant as Father to son: 'When Israel was a child, I loved him, and out of Egypt I called my son. I said to you, "Let my son go that he may worship me". But you refused to let him go; now I will kill your firstborn son.' (Hos. 11:1).

II. 1 *Jonah prayed to the Lord his God from the belly of the fish*

Chapter two of Jonah is an interlude between the two parts of the parable. It is cast as a prayer of Jonah from the belly of the fish. In fact it is more like a psalm in two parts: a psalm or lament of the Suffering Servant's descent into death or exile; and then, from verse 6b to the end, the Servant's psalm of faith and thanksgiving after restoration and raising up. Since Jonah is able to pray from the belly of the fish, we know that Jonah's death is not intended to be one of personal death and oblivion. Rather we must hear it as the prayer of a people in the depths of Exile coming to terms with the meaning of that Exile and perhaps, even, a penitential psalm of sorts.

We are reminded of that great Psalm of the Exile:

> By the rivers of Babylon, there we sat down, yea, we wept when we remembered Zion. We hung our harps upon the willows in the midst of it. For there those who carried us away captive asked of us a song, and those who plundered us requested mirth, saying, 'Sing us one of the songs of Zion!' How shall we sing the Lord's song in a foreign land?[10]

Another Psalm which is similar in many ways to the lament portion of Jonah's Psalm and which is also suggestive of a lament from the depths of exile is Psalm 88:

> O Lord, God of my salvation, when, at night, I cry out in your presence, let my prayer come before you; incline your ear to my cry. For my soul is full of troubles, and my life draws near to Sheol. I am counted among those who go down to the Pit; I am like those who have no help, like those forsaken among the dead, like the slain that lie in the grave, like those whom you remember no more, for they are cut off from your hand. You have put me in the depths of the Pit, in the regions dark and deep. Your wrath lies heavy upon

10 Ps. 137:1–4.

me, and you overwhelm me with all your waves. Selah. You
have caused my companions to shun me; you have made me
a thing of horror to them. I am shut in so that I cannot
escape; my eye grows dim through sorrow. Every day I call
on you, O Lord; I spread out my hands to you. Do you work
wonders for the dead? Do the shades rise up to praise you?
Selah. Is your steadfast love declared in the grave, or your
faithfulness in Abaddon? Are your wonders known in the
darkness, or your saving help in the land of forgetfulness?
But I, O Lord, cry out to you; in the morning my prayer
comes before you. O Lord, why do you cast me off? Why do
you hide your face from me? Wretched and close to death
from my youth up, I suffer your terrors; I am desperate.
Your wrath has swept over me; your dread assaults destroy
me. They surround me like a flood all day long; from all
sides they close in on me. You have caused friend and neigh-
bour to shun me; my companions are in darkness.[11]

The cry of Jeremiah in his lamentation is yet another
example:

You have made us filth and rubbish among the peoples. All
our enemies have opened their mouths against us; panic and
pitfall have come upon us, devastation and destruction. My
eyes flow with rivers of tears because of the destruction of
my people. My eyes will flow without ceasing, without
respite, until the Lord from heaven looks down and sees. My
eyes cause me grief at the fate of all the young women in my
city. Those who were my enemies without cause have
hunted me like a bird; they flung me alive into a pit and
hurled stones on me; water closed over my head; I said, 'I
am lost'. I called on your name, O Lord, from the depths of
the pit; you heard my plea, 'Do not close your ear to my cry
for help, but give me relief!'[12]

---

11 Ps. 88:1–13 A Song. A Psalm of the Korahites. To the leader: according to Mahalath Leannoth. A Maskil of Heman the Ezrahite. We
find this same theme in the Book of Job and in the Lamentations of
Jeremiah.
12 Lam. 3:45–56.

Though personalized in many cases, all of these are the cries of the remnant of the people of God, struggling with the pain of Exile and seeking to make sense of it while still not charging God with unrighteousness.

II. 2 *saying, 'I called to the Lord out of my distress, and he answered me; out of the belly of Sheol I cried, and you heard my voice.*

Jonah begins the lament portion of his Song from the Depths with two parallel lines, one informing the other. First he 'calls' || 'cries' to the Lord. Since we are informed in Psalm 6:5 that 'in death there is no remembrance of you; who could sing your praises in Sheol?' we assume that the deep into which Jonah is descending is not personal annihilation by death. Rather we hear Jonah speaking here as the exile, searching to make sense of that Exile. There is a similar sense of this cry of anguish to the Lord in Psalm 130:

> Out of the depths I cry to you, O Lord. Lord, hear my voice!
> Let your ears be attentive to the voice of my supplications!
> If you, O Lord, should mark iniquities, Lord, who could
> stand? But there is forgiveness with you, so that you may be
> revered. I wait for the Lord, my soul waits, and in his word
> I hope; my soul waits for the Lord more than those who
> watch for the morning, more than those who watch for the
> morning. O Israel, hope in the Lord! For with the Lord there
> is steadfast love, and with him is great power to redeem. It
> is he who will redeem Israel from all its iniquities.[13]

We should note too that the anguish is associated with a sense of sin and iniquity, and the cry for deliverance is associated with repentance and a cry for mercy. This is an important consideration as noted above.

It is possible that psalms such as these might also be associated with the liturgy of the Day of Atonement and with

13 Ps. 130:1 – 131:1.

the High Priest's penitential preparations for the sacrifice after the Exile and during the time of the Second Temple.[14] We have suggested that Jonah is acting as a kind of High Priest for the foreign sailors – the Gentiles – and it is not surprising that a high priestly lamentation should be on his lips in this instance of his sacrifice.

The phrase 'out of my distress' is parallel to 'out of the belly of Sheol'. Sheol is used here interchangeably with the great fish which swallows up Jonah. In its basic meaning Sheol is 'the bottom' or 'the furthest down'. It is 'the depths'. When used with a vertical spatial sense it is the opposite of 'heaven':

> Can you find out the deep things of God? Can you find out the limit of the Almighty? It is higher than heaven – what can you do? Deeper than Sheol – what can you know? Its measure is longer than the earth, and broader than the sea.[15]

Sheol is a metaphoric and poetic word which defies strict definition. When it is associated with water as it is here, Sheol is the depths of the sea, river or swamp – the very bottom. When associated with land it is the very depths of the underworld and by extension the grave itself, whether it be the tomb in the cave or in the ground. In some translations it is associated with hell, though biblical hell is really the chaos preceding creation. In less physical terms it can also be the depths of the spirit, as in 'the anguish of the soul' or 'depression'. It is sometimes understood as isolation, even isolation from God. Often it is a condition of unawareness of the normal world of life, though whether or not it is unconsciousness is not clear. It is said that God cannot be praised or glorified in Sheol:

14 Certainly, in his preparations for the great sacrifice on the Day of Atonement, the High Priest was required to stand barefoot on the pavement all night and read (or have read to him) the Books of Job, Ezra and the Chronicles, all of which contain this same sort of penitential psalmody. (*Mishna*, Yoma 1:6)

15 Job 11:7–9.

For Sheol cannot thank you, death cannot praise you; those who go down to the Pit cannot hope for your faithfulness. The living, the living, they thank you, as I do this day; fathers make known to children your faithfulness.[16]

The Psalms often use Sheol to describe Exile.

The descent into Sheol, often mistranslated or misunderstood as a/the descent into hell, does often describe the person in the process of dying or at least gravely ill and suffering. Certainly it presumes utter helplessness, and as such, suggests a turning to outside help, usually the Lord. 'Lord, I can no longer help myself; please save me and have mercy on me!' So in our verse, Jonah calls out of his grave distress as he sinks into the bowels of the sea for his God to help him.

II. 3 *You cast me into the deep, into the heart of the seas, and the flood surrounded me; all your waves and your billows passed over me.*

There is just the merest hint of 'poor me!' in this verse. 'I'm just a simple, nice person, God-fearing and decent. Now look what you've got me into.' Yet we are reminded here of the sailors' faithful statement: 'All of this is your set purpose, O Lord.' While Jonah offered himself to be sacrificed in the sea, yet the principle of 'the one for the many' is God's own formula for the forgiveness of sin; but it does raise a conflict in the sacrificial victim between human ego and divine plan, to which Jesus' own struggle on the Mount of Olives bears eloquent testimony. Thus Jonah makes it clear: 'You cast me into the deep'; this is the Lord's doing and it is a marvel in our eyes.

The image is one of sinking into the water and perhaps even drowning. We find it described elsewhere in the Psalms:

16 Isa. 38:18–19.

Deep calls to deep at the thunder of your cataracts; all your waves and your billows have gone over me.[17]

Save me, God, for the waters have closed in on my very being. I am sinking in the deepest swamp and there is no firm ground. I have stepped into deep water and the waves are washing over me. I am exhausted with calling out, my throat is hoarse, my eyes are worn out with searching for my God. More numerous than the hairs of my head are those who hate me without reason. Those who seek to get rid of me are powerful, my treacherous enemies. (Must I give back what I have never stolen?) God, you know how foolish I am, my offences are not hidden from you. Those who hope in you must not be made fools of, Yahweh Sabaoth, because of me! Those who seek you must not be disgraced, God of Israel, because of me! It is for you I bear insults, my face is covered with shame: I am estranged from my brothers, alienated from my own mother's sons; for I am eaten up with zeal for your house, and insults directed against you fall on me. I mortify myself with fasting, and find myself insulted for it, I dress myself in sackcloth and become their laughing-stock, the gossip of people sitting at the gate, and the theme of drunkards' songs. And so, I pray to you, Yahweh, at the time of your favour; in your faithful love answer me, in the constancy of your saving power. Rescue me from the mire before I sink in; so I shall be saved from those who hate me, from the watery depths. Let not the waves wash over me, nor the deep swallow me up, nor the pit close its mouth on me. Answer me, Yahweh, for your faithful love is generous; in your tenderness turn towards me; do not turn away from your servant, be quick to answer me, for I am in trouble. Come to my side, redeem me, ransom me because of my enemies. You know well the insults, the shame and disgrace I endure. Every one of my oppressors is known to you. Insult has broken my heart past cure. I hoped for sympathy, but in vain, for consolers – not one to be found. To eat they gave me poison, to drink, vinegar when I was thirsty.[18]

17 Ps. 42:7.
18 Ps. 69:1–21.

Psalm 42 seems to suggest the waters of a river with cataracts, perhaps the Nile or the Jordan, and an experience of passing through them – intimations of the 'passings-over' through the deep in Israel's past experience. Psalm 69, while a much more personal lament of the kind we hear in Jeremiah's woes, likens the deep to a swamp, perhaps the Sea of Reeds of the Passover. In both cases, as well as the case with Jonah, we hear a cry from Israel's exiles and an echo of the passion of Jesus on the cross.

In Psalm 69 there is also a suggestion of Jonah's initial reaction to the Lord's commission to preach repentance to the 'evil empire' of Assyria and its capital, Nineveh:

> May their own table prove a trap for them, and their abundance a snare; may their eyes grow so dim that they cannot see, all their muscles lose their strength. Vent your fury on them, let your burning anger overtake them. Reduce their encampment to ruin, and leave their tents untenanted, for hounding someone you had already stricken, for redoubling the pain of one you had wounded. Charge them with crime after crime, exclude them from your saving justice, erase them from the book of life, do not enrol them among the upright.[19]

Here is the stark desire for personal or national justice and vengeance in the face of aggression which still besets our nations today. It is a kind of distorted black-and-white view which is often expressed by the affirmation that 'God is on my/our side and I/we will have my/our revenge.' The command 'Love your enemies' is quite clearly not fair on me and mine and is an offence to human justice. Thus we recall again that Peter took out his sword to kill the 'enemies' of Jesus on the Mount of Olives. The parable of Jonah makes it quite clear that God's purposes of redeeming the world transcend my personal need for what's fair – for me! We shall see this same struggle between my justice and God's mercy a little further along in the parable.

19 Ps. 69:22–8.

II. 4 *And I said: 'I am cast out from before your eyes; and I will never see your holy temple again' (or '. . . yet I will see once more your holy temple.')*

Both translations are possible in this verse. If being cast out of the Lord's sight is a parallel of not seeing the temple of God's Presence, we have a lovely play on the word 'to see': 'You no longer see me and thus I no longer can see you.' In this case, there is a kind of hopeless finality about Jonah's condition and we can hear the despair of the exiled Israel about the destruction of the temple (whether in Samaria or, later, in Jerusalem). *'Eloi, Eloi! Lamah sabachthani?'*

The translation which affirms that 'I will see once more your holy temple' is more hopeful and suggests restoration, perhaps more fitting for the verses of 'raising up' which follow this one. In either instance, there are clear indications in this verse that Jonah's descent into the sea is also the descent of the people of God into the pit of Exile.

II. 5 *The waters round me rose to my neck, the deep was closing round me, seaweed twining round my head.*

The image in this verse is one of the rising waters and the sinking Jonah. He is not yet underwater, but in process of drowning and sinking fast. Many translations of this verse follow the Greek and Latin with regard to 'my neck' – that is, they translate it as 'my soul' or 'my spirit'. This gives us an insight into the difficulties of too literal a translation on the one hand and a simplistic interpretation on the other. The Hebrew *nephesh* is literally 'throat', but 'the waters rose up to my throat' do not sound smooth in English. Yet the Hebrew understanding that the breathe of life inheres in the throat is important.[20] Clearly 'the waters are about to overwhelm my breathing process and I am about to drown' is the intent. We do have the idiom in English 'I'm up to my

---

20 So when I sneeze, I exhale my life's breathe and require someone to say: 'God bless you' and thus restore my life.

neck in _____ (work, water, and so on)', meaning 'I'm drowning'; so do they.

The seaweed in this verse is the word for 'reed' or 'rushes'. It is the same word as is used for the Reed (Red) Sea in the Passover narrative and the parting of the waters of the sea. It would be equally possible to read this lament of the sinking into the sea as the lament of Pharaoh, the great enemy of Israel, as the waves overwhelm his chariot and the reeds entwine around his head. To read it this way would be to underscore the Gentile mission which is the real point of the parable and sign of Jonah. This descent into the sea would have been the fate of the sailors on Jonah's ship had he not 'taken the plunge' on their behalf and to save them from destruction.[21] The idea is at least distasteful for those who want only justice for themselves. Perhaps the crown of rushes has the same force as the crown of thorns on the cross, the pontifical mitre of the High Priest who is sacrificial victim.

II. 6a *I went down to the very bottoms [roots] of the mountains; the gates of the nether world barred me in for ever;*

Jonah has reached the bottom of the pit. *Mortuus est*; he has died and there is no hope left. The sacrifice is complete and the life given. The Psalm should end here with THE END writ large. Human expectation is that death is final and for ever. With regard to the Exile, it too is an end to all

---

21 There is a later rabbinic parable which recounts that when the people of Israel had passed through the sea and were singing God's praises on the far side of the sea while Pharaoh and his armies were drowning in the sea, the angels of God picked up the great song of praise and rejoicing for the miracle. God, it recounts, comes out of his place and commands Israel and the angels to cease their singing immediately. 'Why?' they cry out. 'We must sing to you and praise you for this wondrous miracle of salvation!' God replies, 'Do not sing while my children (that is, *the Egyptians*) are drowning in the Reed Sea.' (*Talmud Babli*, Meg. 10b).

that was life in the Land of Promise and of Life. There is no meaning and no intercourse with deity in Exile insofar as Israel is concerned.

> [In] the noontide of my days I must depart; I am consigned to the gates of Sheol for the rest of my years. I said, I shall not see the Lord in the land of the living; I shall look upon mortals no more among the inhabitants of the world. My dwelling is plucked up and removed from me like a shepherd's tent; like a weaver I have rolled up my life; he cuts me off from the loom; from day to night you bring me to an end; I cry for help until morning; like a lion he breaks all my bones; from day to night you bring me to an end. Like a swallow or a crane I clamour, I moan like a dove. My eyes are weary with looking upward. O Lord, I am oppressed; be my security! But what can I say? For he has spoken to me, and he himself has done it.[22]

> ... but you are cast out, away from your grave, like loathsome carrion, clothed with the dead, those pierced by the sword, who go down to the stones of the Pit, like a corpse trampled underfoot.[23]

> I am counted among those who go down to the Pit; I am like those who have no help.[24]

II. 6b *yet you brought up my life from the Pit, O Lord my God.*

This is a radical discontinuity in the psalm; verse 6a in no way leads to or even remotely suggests verse 6b. God's mighty acts are ever a surprise – the Creation itself does not follow naturally from the formless void which preceded it; nothing about Ur of the Chaldees or Abraham's life there suggests God's covenant with him or his successors; Israel's slavery in Egypt suggests not an inkling of the Redemption

22 Isa. 38:10–15a.
23 Isa. 14:19.
24 Ps. 88:4.

to follow; and Israel's plight in the depths of Exile has no seeds or promise of the Return. There is a finality about 'the gates of the nether world (death) bar me in forever' for which there is no remedy or solution. And of course this is the surprise part of the sign of Jonah. Where Adam's power fails, God's can begin. 'My ways are not your ways,' says the Lord; and this fact is also a part of the Sign of Jonah.

So too with the resurrection of Jesus. Nothing about the ministry of Jesus (except his own very veiled allusions) or the cross can prepare us for the resurrection on the third day – it is truly a surprise!

This small portion of a verse tucked away in the Book of Jonah is perhaps the epitome of a statement of the supreme power of the Lord God. Nothing in our experience of being alive is as certain and certainly permanent as death, the end of life as we know it. While Adam was finally given the power to make life in procreation, the power is also limited by mortality. The eating from the Tree of Knowledge did indeed give to Adam the divine power – in addition to all the other powers with which the Lord God had graced him – to make life. But since only God has the power to create worlds and environments for human life to flourish, Adam's creation also means, as a consequence, that Adam must die in order to make room for what he makes. Thus death is built into life to make life sustainable. Adam must endure the supreme 'insult' to his/her own power to which irremediable death puts a full and permanent stop, if only to prevent overpopulation.

Thus when God intervenes in what seems to be the over-whelming power and permanence of death to cause life again, it can only be a divine wonder and surprise. Resur-rection, for that is what we call this intrusion of God into the power of death, is always unexpected and totally contrary to reason and human experience. No wonder the powers of the earth, princes and generals, who can manipulate the power of death, find Resurrection so completely unacceptable; they cannot wield this power. God will always win on this account. The Bible is replete with examples, then, of God and his resurrection-life at war with the 'gods' of this world and their weapons of life-termination and death.

Verse 6a begins, 'I went down'; 6b begins, 'You brought me up'. The end of all my efforts and struggles in life result inevitably to my 'going down'. Only the Lord can cause me to 'come up'.

> O Lord, you brought up my soul from Sheol, restored me to life from among those gone down to the Pit.[25]

> For you do not give me up to Sheol, or let your faithful one see the Pit.[26]

We have already seen that before the Exile Israel's definition of immortality or life after death was defined as the sons of each generation living on the family land and earning their living from it, and remembering their parents' grandparents', great grandparents', and so on, names regularly to keep them alive in their (family) place. Put simply, the Exile put an end to even this hope for immortality through the generations, in that families were broken up and killed, sons conscripted into foreign armies and land allocations destroyed by removal of boundary markers and removal of families from the graves of their forbears. Exile was a death worse than the death of any one individual and worthy of the greatest laments, which indeed, as we have seen, it did occasion.

The idea of God causing a remnant of the people to come out of Exile and return to the land, first as a hope and then as a reality, seems to be the origins of what was later to become the 'doctrine' of resurrection. The pattern of it is: going down (one always goes 'down' when leaving

25 Ps. 30:3.
26 Ps. 16:10.

Jerusalem and the Temple on Mount Zion); sojourning there (usually a time of penitence and purgation); and finally being caused (always by God) to go up or ascend (Mount Zion, the high place of Jerusalem and later, of the whole earth). The verb of resurrection is the causative mode[27] of the verb, 'to cause to go up', where God is always the cause. The pattern is: descent from the land into the pit; a sojourn in the pit; and the 'being raised' from the pit back to the land.

The obvious appearance of this template in Israel's tradition surrounds the events of the Exodus from Egypt. As Jacob/Israel prepared to leave the Promised Land where the great famine held sway, the Lord appeared to him and said:

> I myself will go down with you to Egypt, and I will also bring you up again; and Joseph's own hand shall close your eyes.[28]

The promise is that God will go down with Israel into Egypt and will ultimately bring Israel back to the land. In the meantime, Israel will sojourn in Egypt where there is food and life while famine rages in the rest of the world, much as Noah was protected in the ark while the waters covered everything else. This paradigm is later applied to the experience of the going down into Assyria/Babylon; the hope is that God will, after suitable repentance, once again cause the remnant to return one day.

> Our God is a God of salvation, and to God, the Lord, belongs escape from death. But God will shatter the heads of his enemies, the hairy crown of those who walk in their guilty ways. The Lord said, 'I will bring them back from Bashan, I will bring them back from the depths of the sea.[29]

And you divided the sea before them, so that they passed

---

27 For Hebrew students, the hiphil of עלה.
28 Gen. 46:4.
29 Ps. 68:20-2.

through the sea on dry land, but you threw their pursuers into the depths, like a stone into mighty waters.[30]

Then they remembered the days of old, of Moses his servant. Where is the one who brought them up out of the sea with the shepherds of his flock? Where is the one who put within them his holy spirit, who caused his glorious arm to march at the right hand of Moses, who divided the waters before them to make for himself an everlasting name, who led them through the depths? Like a horse in the desert, they did not stumble. Like cattle that go down into the valley, the spirit of the Lord gave them rest. Thus you led your people, to make for yourself a glorious name. Look down from heaven and see, from your holy and glorious habitation. Where are your zeal and your might? The yearning of your heart and your compassion? They are withheld from me.[31]

Was it not you who dried up the sea, the waters of the great deep; who made the depths of the sea a way for the redeemed to cross over?[32]

An even earlier and certainly more dramatic example of the paradigm is to be found in the parable of Joseph, already mentioned in the previous chapter concerning the number 'three'.[33] We meet Joseph as a comely 17–year-old lad, second to last son of his father's twelve boys, who helps his older brothers with the sheep. He is a keen observer of events and good at reporting, but he uses these God-given talents for his own ends by tattling about the brothers to his father. The father improperly dotes on this lad, to the exclusion of his first-born, Reuben, and the other lads, which of course makes them jealous. Joseph has also been gifted with the ability to interpret dreams, a talent which he also uses against the rest of the family for his own self-aggrandisement. In short, we have a typical but handsome and gifted teenager

30 Neh. 9:11.
31 Isa. 63:11–15.
32 Isa. 51:10.
33 The parable of Joseph is to be found in Gen. 37–50, excluding 38.

who is frightfully spoiled and cannot keep his mouth shut.

In their jealousy his brothers turn against him and plot to remove him from their family. Seizing him in the open field, they throw him into a dry well or pit. This is the first descent of Joseph into hell and there is much weeping on the part of his father when he is led to believe in Joseph's death, saying that he, Israel, would go down to Sheol mourning his son.

The brothers sell Joseph to the Ishmaelite traders on their way down to Egypt. Joseph now undergoes his second descent into hell and he is taken to Egypt and sold to Potiphar, an Egyptian nobleman. We are also assured at this point that, 'the Lord is with Joseph' in this second pit and everything that Joseph did in the service of Potiphar is most successful. He rises to the top of the household of Potiphar.

However, Joseph's great gift of handsomeness once more gets him into trouble. In the course of his service to Potiphar, Joseph finds himself regularly alone in the house with Potiphar's wife, a situation which it is suggested that Joseph might himself have engineered. She attempts to seduce Joseph and when she finds that she cannot, she charges Joseph with rape to her husband. And Joseph falls a third time into the deepest pit of Egypt, Pharaoh's dungeons.

We can imagine the lament of Joseph in the dungeon in the words of King Hezekiah who lies at the point of death and under grave threat of the approaching armies of Babylon:

I said: In the noontide of my days I must depart; I am consigned to the gates of Sheol for the rest of my years. I said, I shall not see the Lord in the land of the living; I shall look upon mortals no more among the inhabitants of the world. My dwelling is plucked up and removed from me like a shepherd's tent; like a weaver I have rolled up my life; he cuts me off from the loom; from day to night you bring me to an end; I cry for help until morning; like a lion he breaks all my bones; from day to night you bring me to an end. Like

a swallow or a crane I clamour, I moan like a dove. My eyes
are weary with looking upward. O Lord, I am oppressed; be
my security! But what can I say? For he has spoken to me,
and he himself has done it. All my sleep has fled because of
the bitterness of my soul. O Lord, by these things people
live, and in all these is the life of my spirit. Oh, restore me
to health and make me live![34]

Again we hear the comforting words: 'And the Lord was
with Joseph'. Sure enough he rises again to the top of this
hell to become assistant to the chief jailer. It is at the very
bottom of this lowest pit that Joseph has his conversion in
the sense that he discovers that his gifts are to be used for
the Lord and not for himself.

Pharaoh's Butler and Baker have been condemned to the
prison and join Joseph there. Each of these two worthies
has a dream. The Butler, whose job has been to handle
Pharaoh's cup of divination, dreams that he sees a vine on
which there are three branches. Each branch grows, flowers
and fruits and the Butler then squeezes the fruit into
Pharaoh's cup. Likewise, the Baker also dreams. He sees
himself with three bread-baskets on his head, the third full
of cakes for Pharaoh. The birds come down and eat the
cakes in the topmost basket. Both men go to Joseph when
they find that he can interpret dreams. Joseph's response,
'Only God can interpret dreams' is the sign of his repentance – this is God's doing and for God's sake, not mine and
for me.

The interpretation for the Butler indicates that in three
days he will be restored to his position with Pharaoh. Sadly
for the Baker, in three days he will be hanged. Joseph asks
the Butler to remember him (for life) to Pharaoh when he
returns to the palace. The Butler forgets, and Joseph must
remain in the pit of Sheol for two more years, presumably
perfecting his humility. We are led to understand that
Joseph remains in the pit for three years, forgotten by all
but the Lord who continues to be 'with Joseph'.

34 Isa. 38:10–16.

Finally the Lord causes Pharaoh, the self-styled 'god' of Egypt, to have a dream touching upon the very welfare of Egypt itself, which Pharaoh and his wise men are unable to interpret. The Butler remembers Joseph, and Joseph's resurrection begins:

> Then Pharaoh sent for Joseph, and he was hurriedly brought up out of the dungeon. When he had shaved himself and changed his clothes, he came in before Pharaoh.
>
> Joseph answered Pharaoh, 'It is not I; God will give Pharaoh a favourable answer ... now therefore let Pharaoh select a man who is discerning and wise, and set him over the land of Egypt.'
>
> Pharaoh said to his servants, 'Can we find anyone else like this – one in whom is the spirit of God?' So Pharaoh said to Joseph, 'Since God has shown you all this, there is no one so discerning and wise as you. You shall be over my house, and all my people shall order themselves as you command; only with regard to the throne will I be greater than you.' And Pharaoh said to Joseph, 'See, I have set you over all the land of Egypt'. Removing his signet ring from his hand, Pharaoh put it on Joseph's hand; he arrayed him in garments of fine linen, and put a gold chain around his neck. He had him ride in the chariot of his second-in-command; and they cried out in front of him, 'Bow the knee!' Thus he set him over all the land of Egypt. Moreover Pharaoh said to Joseph, 'I am Pharaoh, and without your consent no one shall lift up hand or foot in all the land of Egypt.' Pharaoh gave Joseph the name Zaphenath-paneah; and he gave him Asenath daughter of Potiphera, priest of On, as his wife. Thus Joseph gained authority over the land of Egypt. Joseph was thirty years old when he entered the service of Pharaoh king of Egypt. And Joseph went out from the presence of Pharaoh, and went through all the land of Egypt.[35]

In fact, Joseph is given the task now of saving Egypt, some-

---

35 Gen. 41:14,16,33, 38–46.

thing which the 'god' of Egypt cannot do himself. Joseph is raised up to become God's servant and redeem the pagans. Joseph is described in the parable as in the style of Adam at creation. He is given authority over the entire land of Egypt; his word is law. He is laden with signs of his authority – the ring, the golden collar of command, and the linen vestments. He rides in the state chariot and the people cry out: 'Blessed is he who comes in the name of the lord Pharaoh!' Finally, like God to Adam in the beginning, Pharaoh tells him that he is to rule over all the household of Egypt – except in the case of Pharaoh himself, who is, after all, above Joseph still. 'I am Pharaoh', he says, 'and you are my servant'. 'I am the Lord,' says God to Adam, 'and you are my servant'. In all else, both Joseph and Adam are kings of the land. They are king and servant both. The task is salvation. Like Jesus and all Levites, his ministry begins at the age of thirty.

When Joseph's father Israel dies, the brothers fear for their lives over what they have done to Joseph in the past. Joseph's response to them gives us the whole sense of the purposeful nature of the 'going down, the sojourn of repentance and the raising up' paradigm:

> But Joseph said to them, 'Do not be afraid! Am I in the place of God? Even though you intended to do harm to me, God intended it for good, in order to preserve a numerous people, as he is doing today. So have no fear; I myself will provide for you and your little ones.' In this way he reassured them, speaking kindly to them.[36]

The little dramas of our ordinary lives, our small ambitions

---

36 Gen. 50:19–21. The remainder of the story of Joseph, from his ascension to Pharaoh's right hand until the death of his father, is a study of repentance and how Joseph determines whether his brothers have truly repented of their jealousy of him or whether their new behaviour arises solely out of their need for grain. Their willingness to give their lives for their youngest brother and Joseph's full sibling, Benjamin, assures Joseph that, given the same situation with Benamin that confronted them before with Joseph, they are willing now to make a different choice of behaviour. This is true repentance.

and failures, our emotional highs and descents into the pits and sheols of our lives often engage us so completely and passionately that we become deaf to the quiet descant above the line of the plan and purpose of God. We descend (or are thrown) into the dry wells of life and find ourselves languishing there without hope. But sometimes, if we know him or at least have been introduced to him, God and his Tune insinuate themselves into our dungeons and we begin to be converted. We begin to see that our giftedness and talents when abused and used for self have been the very spades that have dug the hole into which we have fallen. Like Joseph, we learn to say, 'Is it not God that interprets dreams?' It is in our humility, obtained through such sorrow, that God finds the handle to cause us to be raised up.

While this parable of Joseph might well be the biblical prototype of the paradigm of fall, languish and be raised, we find evidences throughout Scripture of the same pattern, especially in the writings of the Exile.

> As for you also, because of the blood of my covenant with you, I will set your prisoners free from the waterless pit. Return to your stronghold, O prisoners of hope; today I declare that I will restore to you double.[37]

> For myself, wounded wretch that I am, by your saving power raise me up! I will praise God's name in song, I will extol him by thanksgiving, for this will please Yahweh more than an ox, than a bullock horned and hoofed. The humble have seen and are glad. Let your courage revive, you who seek God. For God listens to the poor, he has never scorned his captive people. Let heaven and earth and seas, and all that stirs in them, acclaim him! For God will save Zion, and rebuild the cities of Judah, and people will live there on their own land; the descendants of his servants will inherit it, and those who love his name will dwell there.[38]

---

37 Zech. 9:11–12. Certainly at the end of the parable of Job we have an example of being restored after the sacrifice with double of what was before.

38 Ps. 69:29–36.

> You who have made me see many troubles and calamities
> will revive me again; from the depths of the earth you will
> bring me up again.[39]

> For great is your steadfast love toward me; you have deliv-
> ered my soul from the depths of Sheol.[40]

We have remarked briefly upon the indications in this
parable – and thus all those akin to it – that resurrection, as
unexpected and undeserved as it is, is always purposive.
God raises those in death because he has a purpose for
them. In the case of Joseph it was so that he could save the
many,[41] including the Gentile Pharaoh and his Egyptians as
well as his own people, from death. We shall see that same
purpose in the parable of Jonah further along.

There is a temptation to see resurrection in personal and
selfish terms and as a reward for good living. Unfortunately for such a view, God is more practical and his plan
far more global and universal. The repentance that occurs
in the languishing portion of the paradigm is to move me
from using the gifts he has given me for his purposes rather
than my own gain. Resurrection re-equips me for his
mission!

> Create in me a clean heart, O God, and put a new and right
> spirit within me. Do not cast me away from your presence,
> and do not take your holy spirit from me. Restore to me the
> joy of your salvation, and sustain in me a willing spirit.
> Then I will teach transgressors your ways, and sinners will
> return to you.[42]

---

39 Ps. 71:20.
40 Ps. 86:13.
41 For Hebrew scholars and Catholic liturgists 'the many' = הרבים in the
   sense of 'the congregation of the faithful', used later in the Manual of
   Discipline of the Dead Sea Scrolls Covenanters.
42 Ps. 51:10–13.

II. 7 *As my life was ebbing away, I remembered the Lord; and my prayer came to you, into your holy temple.*

Here is a description of the dynamic of the languishing phase of the paradigm. It is the movement from the idolatry of self to repentance. The acknowledgement of being upon the brink of death and being unable to do anything about it becomes the incentive to look beyond self for help. Because my life is ebbing away I remember the Lord and call out to him in his Holy Place. 'To remember' is more powerful in Hebrew than in English in the sense that English is only a thought to the past whereas in Hebrew 'to remember' calls to present reality. For those familiar with the Twelve Steps of Alcoholics Anonymous this movement from self to Someone greater is precisely the movement from Step One and its acknowledgement of helplessness and being at the very bottom of the pit, to Step Two and the acceptance of a Higher Power outside of and beyond self.[43] It is the movement from fear to faith.

The story is told of the martyrdom of the great Rabbi Akiba by the Roman authorities. Akiba was sentenced to have his flesh peeled from his body while still alive. As the excruciatingly painful procedure was begun, Akiba cried out the words of the Shema, 'Hear, O Israel, the Lord is our God and He alone!' His disciples standing nearby could not believe that in this moment of terrible pain and impending death their master could have the presence to affirm his belief in a God who seemed to have abandoned him. They questioned him about it, and he taught them: 'The pain is only momentary and my life is ending. By remembering the Name of God now, when I have gone I leave God present in my place.'

43 Step 1: 'We admitted we were powerless over alcohol – that our lives had become unmanageable'. Step 2: 'We came to believe that a Power greater than ourselves could restore us to sanity.' *Alcoholics Anonymous (The Big Book)* (A.A. General Service Office, Stonebow, York:) 3rd edn, p. 59.

Likewise we remember Jesus, beset by fear in the Garden of Gethsemane, when he moves from that fear to faith: 'Not my will, but Thine be done.' And again as he confronts death on the cross: 'Father, into Your hands I commit my spirit!' No matter that the sacrifice is for others; the fear and its conversion are very personal.

The 'holy temple' mentioned here should be understood as God's own place, his 'Holy Habitation on high' and not a particular temple such as the one in Jerusalem or on Gerizim.

II. 8 *Those who pay regard to [remember or rely upon] vain idols abandon their [hope of] mercy.*

We might translate this verse: 'Those who, in matters of life and death, remember or rely upon vain idols – extensions of self – abandon the choice of faith or reliance upon God and thus lose all chance of his mercy or steadfast love'. This verse resonates with the earlier narrative in the parable, where the sailors cry out to their gods for help in the storm and find no help:

> Then the men feared the Lord even more, and they offered a sacrifice to the Lord and made vows ...

is parallel to Jonah's own declaration:

> But I with the voice of thanksgiving will sacrifice to you; what I have vowed I will pay. Deliverance belongs to the Lord!

Jonah's first declaration as the Lord raises him from the deep is a statement of simple faith, the faith of Israel. While the nations of the earth worship many and diverse gods, there is no hope in these gods for life in the face of death. The prophet Isaiah reflects on this same declaration of Israel's faith:

> Truly, you are a God who hides himself, O God of Israel, the Saviour. All of them are put to shame and confounded,

the makers of idols go in confusion together. But Israel is saved by the Lord with everlasting salvation; you shall not be put to shame or confounded to all eternity. For thus says the Lord, who created the heavens (he is God!), who formed the earth and made it (he established it; he did not create it a chaos, he formed it to be inhabited!): I am the Lord, and there is no other.[44]

And implicit in this affirmation of the faith of Israel is the burden for which Israel has been chosen in making the Lord God known to those who do not know him and thus cannot enjoy his mercy and loving-kindness. Isaiah continues by declaring God's purposes for an Israel raised up from exile and his plan for the world:

Assemble yourselves and come together, draw near, you survivors of the nations! They have no knowledge, those who carry about their wooden idols, and keep on praying to a god that cannot save. Declare and present your case; let them take counsel together! Who told this long ago? Who declared it of old? Was it not I, the Lord? There is no other god besides me, a righteous God and a Saviour; there is no one besides me. Turn to me and be saved, all the ends of the earth! For I am God, and there is no other. By myself I have sworn, from my mouth has gone forth in righteousness a word that shall not return: 'To me every knee shall bow, every tongue shall swear'.[45]

Implicit also in the comparison of Israel's faith in one God to the fruitless worship of the gods of the nations is the principle of free choice. The nations could have access to the Lord if they would but repent. God is not out of bounds for them but accessible if somehow he can be made known to them. We shall see further along how Jonah's sense of justice for himself would deny the mercy of God to the nations. This is precisely what Jesus meant by the cleansing of the Temple. There are still extant signs which were

44 Isa. 45:15–18.
45 Isa. 45:20–3.

posted on the Temple outer walls: 'Gentiles! Do not enter!'
Jesus declares: 'My house shall be called a house of prayer
for all the nations; you have made it a denominational
fortress.'[46] Jesus is simply quoting and applying what he
has read, again in Isaiah the prophet:

> And the foreigners who join themselves to the Lord, to minis-
> ter to him, to love the name of the Lord, and to be his
> servants, all who keep the sabbath, and do not profane it, and
> hold fast my covenant – these I will bring to my holy moun-
> tain, and make them joyful in my house of prayer; their burnt
> offerings and their sacrifices will be accepted on my altar; for
> my house shall be called a house of prayer for all peoples.[47]

Just as Israel's relationship with the Lord is predicated upon
the freedom to choose or not choose him, so the Gentiles
also enjoy that choice. That Israel has enjoyed the choice
since the making of the covenant with God at Sinai is clear
from Moses' reiteration of the Law towards the end of the
wanderings in the wilderness:

> I call heaven and earth to witness against you today that I
> have set before you life and death, blessings and curses.
> Choose life so that you and your descendants may live.[48]

When Israel had taken up residence in the land, the choice
continued to be theirs:

> Now if you are unwilling to serve the Lord, choose this day
> whom you will serve, whether the gods your ancestors

46 Mark 11:17.
47 Isa. 56:6–7.
48 Deut. 30:19. Israel's regular reading and reaffirming the covenant in
    earliest times took the form of recitation of choices or options. Six
    Tribes stood on Mount Ebal and six on Mount Gerizim. The Ark was
    set in the plain between the two hills, supported by the priests and
    levites. The terms of the covenant were then read as choices – 'blessed
    are you if you do it; cursed if you do not'. (Josh. 8:33) Jesus' Sermon
    on the Plain, the so-called Beatitudes (Luke 6 and 7), follows the
    same pattern.

served in the region beyond the River or the gods of the
Amorites in whose land you are living; but as for me and my
household, we will serve the Lord.[49]

It should be evident that Israel's understanding of God as
the Creator of everything means that ultimately there is
nothing in creation which can be offered to God which he
does not already own by reason of having made it. The gift
of choice-making freely with which the Lord has gifted
Adam/humankind from the very beginning indicates the one
thing that can be offered to the Lord which he does not
already possess – humankind's free choice of him over all
other gods of this world. Thus when the sinner repents and
turns from him/herself back to God, all heaven rejoices
more than over anything else. Perhaps this is what drives
God to want the repentance of the nations of the world:
'Just so, I tell you, there will be more joy in heaven over one
sinner who repents than over ninety-nine righteous persons
who need no repentance'.[50]

During the time before the Exile in Babylon, Jeremiah the
prophet reminds the people again of the choice of the Lord and
his Way in terms of the blessings and curses when he says:

Thus says the Lord: Cursed are those who trust in mere
mortals and make mere flesh their strength, whose hearts
turn away from the Lord. They shall be like a shrub in the
desert, and shall not see when relief comes. They shall live in
the parched places of the wilderness, in an uninhabited salt
land. Blessed are those who trust in the Lord, whose trust is
the Lord. They shall be like a tree planted by water, sending
out its roots by the stream. It shall not fear when heat comes,
and its leaves shall stay green; in the year of drought it is not
anxious, and it does not cease to bear fruit.[51]

Now the nations might argue that since they did not have
Moses and the prophets, this choice was really not available

49 Josh. 24:15.
50 Luke 15:7.
51 Jer. 17:5–8.

to them; how indeed could they choose the Lord and his Way since they did not know him? It has been said, however, that ignorance is no excuse and that since all humankind is descended from Adam, they should have had some inkling of the choice available to them. We recall again St Paul's argument made most pointedly in his letter to the Romans:

> For the wrath of God is revealed from heaven against all ungodliness and wickedness of those who by their wickedness suppress the truth. For what can be known about God is plain to them, because God has shown it to them. Ever since the creation of the world his eternal power and divine nature, invisible though they are, have been understood and seen through the things he has made. So they are without excuse; for though they knew God, they did not honour him as God or give thanks to him, but they became futile in their thinking, and their senseless minds were darkened. Claiming to be wise, they became fools; and they exchanged the glory of the immortal God for images resembling a mortal human being or birds or four-footed animals or reptiles. Therefore God gave them up in the lusts of their hearts to impurity, to the degrading of their bodies among themselves, because they exchanged the truth about God for a lie and worshipped and served the creature rather than the Creator, who is blessed forever! Amen.[52]

Perhaps this makes the desire of God to extend his salvation to the Gentiles more extraordinary, wonderful and powerful. Such persistence, long-suffering and patience can only be based on God's passion for and rejoicing over the repentant sinner, in receiving that which he did not create and does not have except it be given to him by humankind.

At this point we must pause to consider another liturgical piece that bears some similarity to this Hymn of Jonah in chapter 2. This is the Psalm of David remembered at the close of the story of David's reign in 2 Samuel 22:1ff: 'David spoke to the Lord the words of this song on the day when the Lord delivered him from the hand of all his

52 Rom. 1:18–25.

enemies, and from the hand of Saul'. Some of the imagery is similar to the words of Jonah in his encounter with the fish. Certainly the descriptive words of the passion of these two figures utilize the same poetic figures. For example, David sings:

> For the waves of death encompassed me, the torrents of perdition assailed me; the cords of Sheol entangled me, the snares of death confronted me. In my distress I called upon the Lord; to my God I called. From his temple he heard my voice and my cry came to his ears.[53]

Even the suggestion of resurrection might be said to be similar:

> Then the channels of the sea were seen, the foundations of the world were laid bare at the rebuke of the Lord, at the blast of the breath of his nostrils. He reached from on high, he took me, he drew me out of mighty waters.[54]

But it would be a mistake to find a parallel between these two liturgical pieces other than the similarities of a few poetic metaphors. David's song is the victory song of a triumphant warrior attributing success and deliverance from his enemies to his God:

> He said: The Lord is my rock, my fortress, and my deliverer, my God, my rock, in whom I take refuge, my shield and the horn of my salvation, my stronghold and my refuge, my saviour; you save me from violence. I call upon the Lord, who is worthy to be praised, and I am saved from my enemies.[55]

Jonah, on the other hand, has willingly offered himself as a sacrifice for foreigners; enemies do not take centre stage in Jonah.

53 2 Sam. 22:5–7.
54 Ibid. vss. 16–17.
55 Ibid. vss. 2–4.

Again, with David we are left with the feeling that God is simply another part of his arsenal, a kind of secret weapon or *deus ex machina*, as he fights off his enemies:

> Then the earth reeled and rocked; the foundations of the heavens trembled and quaked, because he was angry. Smoke went up from his nostrils, and devouring fire from his mouth; glowing coals flamed forth from him. He bowed the heavens, and came down; thick darkness was under his feet. He rode on a cherub, and flew; he was seen upon the wings of the wind. He made darkness around him a canopy, thick clouds, a gathering of water. Out of the brightness before him coals of fire flamed forth. The Lord thundered from heaven; the Most High uttered his voice. He sent out arrows, and scattered them – lightning, and routed them. Then the channels of the sea were seen, the foundations of the world were laid bare at the rebuke of the Lord, at the blast of the breath of his nostrils.[56]

There is certainly no expression either of the Lord's compassion or his desire to save David's enemies here; we get a sense from David of 'My God is bigger than your god(s), and he will beat you up'.

Furthermore David makes it clear that he has 'won' God's favour and power by being righteous:

> He brought me out into a broad place; he delivered me, because he delighted in me. The Lord rewarded me according to my righteousness; according to the cleanness of my hands he recompensed me. For I have kept the ways of the Lord, and have not wickedly departed from my God. For all his ordinances were before me, and from his statutes I did not turn aside. I was blameless before him, and I kept myself from guilt. Therefore the Lord has recompensed me according to my righteousness, according to my cleanness in his sight.[57]

Clearly, David's 'success' is achieved through a quid pro quo with the Lord and has little or nothing to do with the

---

56 Ibid. vss. 8–16.
57 Ibid. vss. 20–25.

Lord's will; David earned his reward which is his own and has nothing to do with sacrifice, especially on behalf of others, much less his enemies. We can see in the differences between these two psalms the difference between the earlier prophetic religion of Israel and the later monarchial and temporal power-based religion which characterized Jerusalem and Judah in the time of the kings.

In David's words we see the foundations of a power-based, military and political messiahship which is quite different from the sacrificial messiahship of the High Priesthood established in the wilderness with Aaron and his house:

> With the loyal you show yourself loyal; with the blameless you show yourself blameless; with the pure you show yourself pure, and with the crooked you show yourself perverse. You deliver a humble people, but your eyes are upon the haughty to bring them down. Indeed, you are my lamp, O Lord, the Lord lightens my darkness. By you I can crush a troop, and by my God I can leap over a wall. This God – his way is perfect; the promise of the Lord proves true; he is a shield for all who take refuge in him. For who is God, but the Lord? And who is a rock, except our God? The God who has girded me with strength has opened wide my path. He made my feet like the feet of deer, and set me secure on the heights. He trains my hands for war, so that my arms can bend a bow of bronze. You have given me the shield of your salvation, and your help has made me great. You have made me stride freely, and my feet do not slip; I pursued my enemies and destroyed them, and did not turn back until they were consumed. I consumed them; I struck them down, so that they did not rise; they fell under my feet. For you girded me with strength for the battle; you made my assailants sink under me. You made my enemies turn their backs to me, those who hated me, and I destroyed them. They looked, but there was no one to save them; they cried to the Lord, but he did not answer them. I beat them fine like the dust of the earth, I crushed them and stamped them down like the mire of the streets. You delivered me from strife with the peoples; you kept me as the head of the

nations; people whom I had not known served me. Foreigners came cringing to me; as soon as they heard of me, they obeyed me. Foreigners lost heart, and came trembling out of their strongholds. The Lord lives! Blessed be my rock, and exalted be my God, the rock of my salvation, the God who gave me vengeance and brought down peoples under me, who brought me out from my enemies; you exalted me above my adversaries, you delivered me from the violent. For this I will extol you, O Lord, among the nations, and sing praises to your name. He is a tower of salvation for his king, and shows steadfast love to his anointed, to David and his descendants forever.[58]

While David suggests humility as a virtue which appeals to the Lord, he does not here seem to be much possessed of that virtue himself. It is no wonder that Jesus later in no way associates himself with this kind of messiah, but invokes the humble title of Son of Man for himself as he prepares himself, not for the overthrow of the temporal power of Rome, but for the sacrifice for the salvation of all the nations.[59]

II. 9 *But I with the voice of thanksgiving will sacrifice to you; what I have vowed I will pay. Deliverance belongs to the Lord!*

This verse provides a kind of coda to Jonah's psalm of travail in the fish. We can perhaps compare it to the Song of Miriam and the Children of Israel once they have passed through the waters in safety:

> Then Moses and the Israelites sang this song to the Lord: 'I will sing to the Lord, for he has triumphed gloriously; horse and rider he has thrown into the sea. The Lord is my strength and my might, and he has become my salvation;

---

58 Ibid. vss. 26–51.
59 Cf. John 3:16–17.

this is my God, and I will praise him, my father's God, and
I will exalt him.'[60]

The song extolling the triumph of the Lord over the tribu-
lation and death of his people by bringing them through the
deep to new life is certainly as appropriate here for Jonah as
it was to Moses and Miriam. It is a proclamation of the
Lord's ability to overcome even the permanence of death
itself. We find the same sentiment in the Revelation of John
in the song of those who have come through the great tribu-
lation of the end times and are redeemed:

After this I looked, and there was a great multitude that no
one could count, from every nation, from all tribes and
peoples and languages, standing before the throne and
before the Lamb, robed in white, with palm branches in
their hands. They cried out in a loud voice, saying, 'Salvation belongs to our God who is seated on the throne, and to
the Lamb!' And all the angels stood around the throne and
around the elders and the four living creatures, and they fell
on their faces before the throne and worshipped God,
singing, 'Amen! Blessing and glory and wisdom and thanksgiving and honour and power and might be to our God
forever and ever! Amen.' Then one of the elders addressed
me, saying, 'Who are these, robed in white, and where have
they come from?' I said to him, 'Sir, you are the one that
knows.' Then he said to me, 'These are they who have come
out of the great ordeal; they have washed their robes and
made them white in the blood of the Lamb. For this reason
they are before the throne of God, and worship him day and
night within his temple, and the one who is seated on the
throne will shelter them. They will hunger no more, and
thirst no more; the sun will not strike them, nor any scorching heat; for the Lamb at the centre of the throne will be
their shepherd, and he will guide them to springs of the
water of life, and God will wipe away every tear from their
eyes.'[61]

60 Exod. 15:1–2.
61 Rev. 7:9–17.

Our translation places Jonah's sacrifice and payment of vows in the future: 'I will sacrifice; I will pay my vows.' Both verbs, however, are in the imperfect in the Hebrew and could be translated: 'I am sacrificing and paying my vows'. In this case, Jonah has not only called the sailors to repentance but also paid the outstanding price of their redemption with his own self-offering, 'Take me, bind me and throw me overboard'. He is indeed sacrificing – his own life for others, the high-priestly oblation. If this is so, perhaps we get a glimmer of Israel's own accommodation to the Exile. Why has the Lord sent them into Exile? Not just for punishment, but for the purpose of driving them to mission in order to save others.

It is perilous to attempt to read the mind of another, much less the mind of Jesus. Yet we cannot help wondering if, when he reads this verse of Jonah and preaches on the sign of Jonah, he hears his own name: 'Deliverance', 'salvation', '*yeshuatha*'[62] is the Lord's or belongs to the Lord. How very disturbing to think that you might have to be the object of the terrified petition of a world caught in hell: 'What shall we do with you to make the sea go down?'

II. 10 *Then the Lord spoke to the fish, and it spewed Jonah out upon the dry land.*

This is the mirror image of what we read in II.2 But the Lord provided a large fish to swallow up Jonah; and Jonah was in the belly of the fish three days and three nights. As the Lord provided the fish to begin with, now he provides the exit from the fish.[63] This verse brings an end to the first reading of the Parable of Jonah and brings us right back to where we began.

---

62 יְשׁוּעָתָה לַיהוָה

63 I am always reminded by Jonah's sojourn in the fish of Pinocchio's adventures in Monstro, the whale in the wonderful story by Carlo Collodi; somehow, Disney's portrayal was never too difficult to appropriate when I was a child, and it remains with me still.

Chapter Three

Because chapter two ends where we began this parable, it is tempting to expect the drama to be finished. We have been told of the mission which God lays upon Jonah, the task of preaching repentance to a people who are not only foreign to Israel but also the arch-enemies of the people whom God has chosen. We have felt the struggle of Jonah to come to terms with this mission and the apparent unfairness of God in proposing forgiveness and salvation to a people who have brought catastrophe on the elect. We know the conviction of Jonah and the people he represents that the Lord only speaks his Word in the 'temple' which is the entire land of Israel – a national prejudice that is finally projected back upon the Almighty as though such a nonsense were his choice.

National prejudice arises among a monotheistic people when the will of the state or its leaders becomes conflated with the will of God. This is never a problem for peoples who have a pantheon of gods, a polytheistic people, for the conflicting wills of many deities are so complex as to render the whole notion of 'divine will' a nonsense. In fact, polytheistic peoples must rely on heroes and national will and purpose from the outset, seeking support from the favourite gods or from magic but never consulting the gods for direction.

Israel, on the other hand, is radically monotheist from the beginning and called to be servants of the divine plan which is revealed to them from time to time, rather than having a national plan which is then projected upon deity. God precedes the nation, its peoples and its leaders, for God was there before the beginning and the entire creation is his. Israel is called to be a people in the first place by God rather than discovering the gods along the way of national life and experience. The real heroes of Israel are not military or social leaders but those who are called by God to reveal him and his purposes; and their chief and most appealing quality to God is humility.

The God of Israel is therefore an inconvenient and awkward deity. By reason of his creation of the world alone there is an assurance that the purpose of that creation and its unfolding in time and place are always subject to his will. He transcends even humankind by reason of having created Adam. Having gifted Adam, i.e. humankind, with his own image and likeness in order to serve him and to care for that creation, Adam always has the potential of a will and plan of his own. The awkwardness of God is that his will must always be first and must prevail. This notion is inherent in Israel's declaration of faith, the Shema: 'Listen, Israel, the Lord is our God and he is alone [transcendent and above and before the creation]; therefore you shall love him [be committed to him and his Way] with all your heart.'

From the expulsion of Adam from the garden in Genesis, the will of God is shown to be the redemption of his creation and its peoples. To accomplish this he enlists a particular people, beginning with Abraham and expanding the operation, the mission, with a people he brings up out of Egypt at the hand of Moses. As with Adam in the beginning, the entire purpose of this particular people is to serve God and make him known in the world. With this God, chosenness and particularity, far from being honorifics, are always purposive and are always couched in terms of service to accomplish his will and purpose. Since the alienation of humankind from the Lord, the service to God is defined as redeeming the nations of the world from their idolatrous alienations to the gods of human self-extension, with the attendant fear and death. From the beginnings with Abraham ('Get up and go . . .') through the directive of Jesus to his disciples ('Get up and go into all the world and preach the good news of the Kingdom . . .') the purpose of the people of God, called by God and responsive to his will, is to be understood as mission – to get back God's world for him.

A problem arises when the chosen people begin to think of their chosenness as divine favouritism bestowing a special status rather than a service. With the people of Israel this problem arose soon after the departure from the land of Egypt. God had led them to the foot of Mount Sinai where Moses directed them to wait while he climbed the mountain to consult with God about the Lord's further plans. To wait without certainty about the future is most difficult, especially in uncomfortable circumstances. The waiting led to a fear that Moses had abandoned them and that they would perish in the wilderness. Fear is, of course, the opposite of faith; and anxiety becomes the seedbed for sin.[1]

The people of Israel call upon Moses' brother Aaron to make for them a visible and tangible image of the Lord to allay their fears, which he does. The sin of the golden calf is Israel's fundamental and original Sin as a missionary people, and it takes a great deal of Moses' efforts to turn away the punishment of the people. And it marks the establishment of the High Priesthood under Aaron for the annual atonement for Sin on the principle which we also have seen in Jonah: 'Take my life instead of theirs'.

While this sin of the golden calf is not national prejudice per se, it does reflect the root of the struggle between Israel

---

1 The concluding prayer of the Pater Noster in the Mass before the doxology recognizes the problem of anxiety and sin: 'Deliver us, Lord, from every evil, and grant us peace in our day. In your mercy keep us free from sin and protect us from all anxiety as we wait in joyful hope for the coming of our Saviour, Jesus Christ.'

and the Lord God. In times of fear and trial, will the people rely on the fidelity of their God or will they turn to themselves and rely on their own efforts and the gods of their own making? Will the fear for national security replace the risky and not altogether clear or certain reliance upon the plan of the Lord?

Perhaps the clearest move of Israel towards national pride and prejudice occurs in the seemingly endless struggles with the Philistines once Israel has taken possession of the land promised them by the Lord. Military setbacks suggest to the people that Philistine successes arise from their having strong military and political leadership in the person of their king. Thus the people of Israel prevail upon the Lord's prophet Samuel to anoint a king for Israel as well:

> Then all the elders of Israel gathered together and came to Samuel at Ramah, and said to him, 'You are old and your sons do not follow in your ways; appoint for us, then, a king to govern us, like other nations'. But the thing displeased Samuel when they said, 'Give us a king to govern us'. Samuel prayed to the Lord, and the Lord said to Samuel, 'Listen to the voice of the people in all that they say to you; for they have not rejected you, but they have rejected me from being king over them. Just as they have done to me, from the day I brought them up out of Egypt to this day, forsaking me and serving other gods, so also they are doing to you.'[2]

Samuel anointed Saul king but deposed him in very short order when Saul attempted to take over the priestly role for himself as well as the military leadership of the armies of Israel. Saul is supplanted by David, who in his turn attempts to centralize the cult under his control by building a temple. He is frustrated in this attempt by the Lord. As David lay dying, however, his younger son Solomon engineered a coup against his older brother the legitimate heir,

2 1 Sam. 8:4–8.

and, with the aid of Nathan the prophet and Bath Sheba his mother, made himself king and emperor without the Lord's election; overthrew the reigning High Priest of Aaron's line in favour of the local line of Zadok; not only built the Temple but took care of the dedicatory prayers and sacrifices himself; and centralized the cult in support of his own rule. National prejudice can be said to have emerged triumphant with Solomon.

It is clear from the ruling about kings and God's restrictions upon them in the Book of Deuteronomy that Solomon set himself over against the institutions established by God through Moses in the wilderness:

> When you have come into the land that the Lord your God is giving you, and have taken possession of it and settled in it, and you say, 'I will set a king over me, like all the nations that are around me', you may indeed set over you a king whom the Lord your God will choose. One of your own community you may set as king over you; you are not permitted to put a foreigner over you, who is not of your own community. Even so, he must not acquire many horses for himself, or return the people to Egypt in order to acquire more horses, since the Lord has said to you, 'You must never return that way again'. And he must not acquire many wives for himself, or else his heart will turn away; also silver and gold he must not acquire in great quantity for himself. When he has taken the throne of his kingdom, he shall have a copy of this law written for him in the presence of the levitical priests. It shall remain with him and he shall read in it all the days of his life, so that he may learn to fear the Lord his God, diligently observing all the words of this law and these statutes, neither exalting himself above other members of the community nor turning aside from the commandment, either to the right or to the left, so that he and his descendants may reign long over his kingdom in Israel.[3]

3 Deut. 17:14–20.

Solomon does the opposite of every point of this ruling, as do most of his successors who sit on the throne in Jerusalem. This behaviour, contrary to the Law of Moses, represents a clear departure from the humility required by the Lord of those who lead his people according to his plan and purpose. Clearly, it is with Solomon that national prejudice against the nations of the world begins. And unfortunately, the anointing of Solomon as the archetype of the kingly messiah runs counter to the archetype of the high priestly messiah of the line of Aaron. The latter is the servant who gives his life for the relief of sin for the people; the former is the national power leader whose task is to seek the aggrandisement of self and nation. When the choice is given to the people of Jerusalem and Judah between Jesus, whose purpose is to offer his life for the forgiveness of sin, and Jesus bar Abbas, whose goal is the restoration of political and national power, Jesus is chosen as the sacrifice and bar Abbas as the 'king'.

By the time of Jesus, national prejudice against the Gentiles and the fear of national destruction was intense; national prejudice and particularity had turned the Temple and its cult into a goal for preservation rather than a means for meeting with the Almighty.

> But some of them went to the Pharisees and told them what he had done. So the chief priests and the Pharisees called a meeting of the council, and said, 'What are we to do? This man is performing many signs. If we let him go on like this, everyone will believe in him, and the Romans will come and destroy both our holy place and our nation.' But one of them, Caiaphas, who was high priest that year, said to them, 'You know nothing at all! You do not understand that it is better for you to have one man die for the people than to have the whole nation destroyed.' He did not say this on his own, but being high priest that year he prophesied that Jesus was about to die for the nation, and not for the nation only, but to gather into one the dispersed children of God.[4]

4 John 11:46–52.

The sign of Jonah, then, is a pointer against national pride and prejudice, against chosenness for favour and towards Israel's original chosenness for mission. Revenge and aggression must give way to self-sacrifice to achieve God's purpose for his world. Perhaps it continues to be a sign for the Church against self-preservation and self-serving and for a constant renewal of her mission in the world. God's purpose is clear:

> Turn to me and be saved, all the ends of the earth! For I am God, and there is no other. By myself I have sworn, from my mouth has gone forth in righteousness a word that shall not return: 'To me every knee shall bow, every tongue shall swear'. Only in the Lord, it shall be said of me, are righteousness and strength; all who were incensed against him shall come to him and be ashamed. In the Lord all the offspring of Israel shall triumph and glory.[5]

Surely the final goal of the Church is to go out of business when the task is completed. We are, after all, in sales – not management!

III. 1 *The word of the Lord came to Jonah a second time, saying,*

The words are identical to I.1 except for the words 'a second time'. Why does God bother to repeat his first word to Jonah? Perhaps it is because Jonah has still not gone to Nineveh. The liturgy of the redemption of the sailors from every nation at the expense of Jonah's life is established – 'all of this is Thy set purpose' cry the sailors as they bind Jonah in sacrifice into the storm. Yet the acceptable liturgy must now be given the flesh and blood of the actual city of Nineveh. In fact, this second story stands in relationship to the first much as the liturgy of the cross on Good Friday stands in relationship to the meal on Holy Thursday; the

---

5 Isa. 45:22–5.

meal establishes the principles of the liturgy while the cross is the actual accomplishment of the sacrifice.

In the same way we are reminded of Jeremiah the prophet who is told to go to the people of Jerusalem and preach repentance. And while Jeremiah does go, he is continually mocked and abused for his efforts and keeps returning to the Lord to report his failure with the hope that God will relieve him of the responsibility, only to hear the word of the Lord: 'Go tell them again, Jeremiah!'

Throughout Scripture the Lord shows himself to be patient and long-suffering with humankind and its folly. The true servant of the Lord must be as patient as the Lord reveals himself to be. Seen in the larger picture of God's purpose for his creation, the re-sending and re-enabling of his servant gives an added dimension to the notion of resurrection. Resurrection is not, then, a reward for the faithful as much as it is restoring the servant to the starting-block for continued mission. Thus when Jesus emerges from the tomb, he immediately calls together his disciples to continue the mission of the Kingdom of God. Resurrection in this sense is always purposive beyond the simple miracle of it. 'Again' here means that the mission of Jonah has not ended despite his wondrous emergence from the belly of the fish.

Another meaning of 'a second time' may have the effect of intensifying the word of the Lord, much as the doubling of the middle letter of the Hebrew 3–letter verb has the effect of intensifying the action. By doubling his instruction to Jonah, the Lord signifies to Jonah – and to us – how important he considers this work and his intentions that it be carried out.

Finally, there is a literary device in parables to the effect that if something is true in a small matter, how much more true is it in a greater matter of the same sort. It is an argument from the lesser to the greater, from the lighter to the heavier; and Jesus uses the device frequently in his own parables; we will see this device again at the end of our parable of Jonah. Therefore if the liturgy of redemption has worked with a small group of sailors caught in hell, how

much more will it work in Nineveh trapped in the hell of its
own sinfulness.

III. 2 *'Get up, go to Nineveh, that great city, and proclaim to it the message that I tell you.'*

Nineveh, we will learn further along, is 'great' in the sense
of its importance to God, for it is God that calls it great. In
the parable it takes on the status of representative of the
entire world which is alienated from the Lord, the Creator
of all. In other times it would be Thebes, Babylon, Persepo-
lis or Rome – the unredeemed mass of humankind. There is
no lack of contemporary examples!

Notice that the Lord does not give the message to be
proclaimed at the outset of the mission. The participial
form of the verb 'tell' indicates a continuing revelation of
the message as Jonah presents himself in Nineveh. There is
no question that this is to be the Lord's message and not the
prophet's. Abraham was told to leave Ur but advised that
he would be told where he was going only when he actually
arrived at the promised land; there was no map given at the
outset of the journey. And again, when he was instructed to
sacrifice Isaac, he was told that the mountain of sacrifice
would be revealed when he got there. Early Christians are
told that they must not be anxious about what they are to
say in the courts of the world; the Lord will make known at
the time what they are to say. Such a lack of planning
requires a sense of the 'big picture' and a great deal of faith;
it is not for the faint-hearted.

III. 3 *So Jonah set out and went to Nineveh, accord-ing to the word of the Lord. Now Nineveh was an exceedingly large city, a three days' walk across.*

Jonah has at least discovered the universality of the word of
the Lord. There is no attempt this time to escape the word
by leaving the land; the Lord's reach is throughout his
creation and not just in the Promised Land, just as his

concern is for the entirety of his creation and not just for Israel. Perhaps this too is one of the lessons of the first mission and the meaning of 'a second time'. We have a sense here of the immediacy of Jonah's response to the Lord's instruction.[6]

While Nineveh might have been impressive with regard to its size and power in its day, it is unlikely that any city of ancient times would have required a three-day journey across it. Rather we are urged to think of it as the same as the sojourn in the belly of the fish, a three-day descent into Sheol. Nineveh, like hell, is three days deep (or wide), a hellish place, as it said in I:2: ' ... for their wickedness has come up before me'. The journey of Jonah into the city is likened to Jonah's descent into Sheol. But as the old saying goes: 'No cross, no crown; nothing ventured, nothing gained.'

III. 4 *Jonah began to go into the city, going a day's walk. And he cried out, 'Forty days more, and Nineveh shall be overthrown!'*

Jonah's is a peripatetic proclamation, made 'on the hoof' so to speak. There is no attempt to find a pulpit or public gathering place. Rather, he preaches on the move, without plan and leaving the results to follow as they may. We are reminded here of Jesus' parable of the Sower.[7] Just as the farmer is not to be concerned that some of the seed falls on weeds, on the path or on stony ground and will not grow, but to scatter liberally and without plan, so Jonah is simply to proclaim the word and to leave the matter of growth, yield and harvest to the Lord.

Clearly the message is not one of simple prediction about

---

6 The Gospel of Mark, especially in the beginning chapters, constantly refers to Jesus' action and movements with the adverb 'immediately', probably with the same idea of the speedy response to the divine imperative for mission now shown by Jonah.

7 Mark 4:3–9 ‖ Luke 8:5–8.

Nineveh's overthrow. Unspoken but clear is the contingency of repentance: 'Forty days more, and Nineveh will be overthrown – if they do not repent'. The fact that they do repent further along makes it clear that repentance is really the issue and the force of the proclamation. We should also note that the five words of Jonah's prophecy represent the shortest prophetic proclamation in the Bible; though Jesus' own proclamation, 'Repent, for the Kingdom of Heaven is at hand' is not much longer. And they have forty days in which to make this decision.

The number forty appears so often in Scripture as a discrete time of some type of duration for change as to make us wonder at the origin and meaning of this number. Some commentators have suggested that it is a large, round number with no particular significance. Yet fifty or a hundred are larger and as round. Surely the fact that the flood lasted forty days in the time of Noah, that Moses was forty days on the mountain, that Israel was forty years in the wilderness, that Elijah was forty days in the cave, that Jesus was forty days in the wilderness and that the Church keeps forty days of Lent demands a better explanation for this particular number than that it is simply a large, round number.

The solution, I think, is to be found at the end of the Book of Genesis at the death of Jacob/Israel in Egypt:

> Joseph commanded the physicians in his service to embalm his father. So the physicians embalmed Israel; they spent forty days in doing this, for that is the time required for embalming. And the Egyptians wept for him seventy days.[8]

For the ancient Egyptians, the time from the death of a person and the going forth of his *ka* (soul) until the weighing of his heart against the feather of *ma'at* (truth/order) to determine whether he might enter the gates of eternity was the length of time it took to embalm or mummify his body. As we see from the case of Jacob/Israel, this process took

8 Gen. 50:2–3.

forty days. Thus forty here probably takes on the sense of the duration from the going out from one condition until the entry into another; it seems often to end with some sort of a conversion. Thus Israel's going out from Egypt and its sins to the passing through the waters of the Jordan into the promised land required forty – years in this case. And so Nineveh has forty days to exit its condition of sinfulness and to enter a condition of salvation from God's punishment. Forty days is given for repentance leading to life or continued stubbornness of heart leading to death. Forty is the time of testing and is the time of the Tempter, the Satan, and the struggle to overcome him.[9]

III. 5 *And the people of Nineveh believed God; they proclaimed a fast, and everyone, great and small, put on sackcloth.*

Wonder of wonders, the Ninevites received the word of the Lord! We note that it does not say that they believed Jonah; rather, it says they believed God. Such a sudden conversion of this great city is truly counterintuitive and defies explanation unless we understand what God knows, that the wickedness and fear of the world are truly discomfiting and suggests some need of the sinful to change so quickly and so radically.

Could there have been some fear such as afflicted the sailors in the first story that drives Nineveh to repentance? In a superb monograph at the beginning of his commentary on Genesis, E. A. Speiser[10] suggests that Abraham was moved to leave Ur of the Chaldees at God's first suggestion to him, not because he was particularly moved by the Lord so much as he was fed up with the gods of his homeland.

---

9 The Lent after death which the Church calls purgatory must surely be reckoned in forties or compounds of forty!

10 E.A. Speiser, 'The Biblical Process' in Genesis, Vol. 1 in *The Anchor Bible Commentary* (Doubleday & Co., Inc. Garden City, N.Y. 1964), pp. xvii–lxxvi.

The gods of Ur, as with the gods of the nations, were plural, capricious and offered nothing that was secure for the future. They were born, made love, fought with each other and with humankind and finally died just as mortal men and women did. Furthermore they were subject to magic themselves and utilized that magic against each other, just as humans did. Speiser suggests that this capricious and uncertain god-system led to Abraham's fear for the future and made him a prime candidate for the Lord's offer of a single God who is faithful and stable. Perhaps it was this kind of gnawing fear that accounts for the repentance and conversion of Nineveh. Certainly Jonah himself has already made such a suggestion in his hymn: 'Those who worship worthless idols forfeit the mercy that could be theirs'.[11]

True repentance and conversion are always a movement from arrogance and pride towards humility. We have said already how much the Lord is desirous of humility as his way into the world. Humility is in fact the very essence of biblical religion and biblical spirituality from the very beginning. Genesis 1:1 begins 'From the outset, God created the heavens and the earth', where God is always the subject and everything else is the object. The humility, that is the dependent nature of the creation upon the author of it, is the principle behind the commandment: 'You shall love the Lord your God with all your heart ...'[12] The very dependence of creation upon its Creator is the meaning of Jesus' saying: 'Let the little children come to me, for of such [as a little child in its total dependence] is the Kingdom of Heaven'.[13] Self-reliance is to make a god out of self and the extensions of self; and when the time comes that self cannot help itself, the fear of death, the ultimate incapacity of the self, enters in and suggests a need to turn (repent) from self to the Creator and to hope for salvation from death. This reliance upon God rather than upon self is called 'faith' and

11 Jonah 2:8.
12 Deut. 6:5.
13 Matt. 19:14.

is the opposite of 'fear'. Humility and faith are inextricably connected, for humility is the emptiness of self.

Humility is, in the prophetic religion of Israel, the only gift that one can bring to God with any meaning, since humility always requires a choice between self and God; for God made everything else and already 'owns' it anyway. Without the virtue of humility, there can be no love, either of another human being or of God. In fact, without humility there can be no other virtues at all. Humility is the only fitting sacrifice to God since it is the sacrifice of self. It is somewhat of a paradox that the only gift I can offer to God is 'nothing' and emptiness of self.[14] The prophet Micah summarizes this sacrifice of self:

> He has told you, O mortal, what is [the] good; and what does the Lord require of you but to do justice, and to love kindness, and to walk humbly with your God?[15]

We understand 'what is good?' in this declaration of Micah as intending 'What is the Good?' where the Good is the same as the Good with which God approved of his creation in the beginning. Since God created the heavens and the earth as a dwelling place for himself, the 'good' of it has the effect of 'good for God to live in', empty and available, and thus holy.

Likewise, when the Lord approaches Cain who is angry and jealous over losing the sacrificing contest with his brother Abel and asks him why he is upset, God reiterates this notion of humility as the Good when he says:

> If you do the Good, will you not be accepted? And if you do not do the Good, sin is lurking at the door; its desire is for you, but you must master it.[16]

In like manner, then, real sin is the exaltation of self, whether with regard to others or, most importantly, to

---

14 The Greek concept is *kenosis*, emptying.
15 Mic. 6:8.
16 Gen. 4:7.

God. In Israel, idolatry is not so much the worship of foreign gods as it is the worship of the extension of self in the form of manufactured idols. The opposite is dependence upon the Lord in humility and a will to service. Thus we have the instance of Moses, of whom it says: 'Now the man Moses was very humble, more so than anyone else on the face of the earth'.[17] Indeed, it was by reason of his humility that the Lord could speak with him 'face to face, as a man speaks with his friend'.

God's initial encounter with Moses is set in humility. Moses, when he first meets the Lord on Mount Sinai in the wilderness while tending the sheep of his father-in-law Jethro, is a runaway murderer from Egypt – certainly not the most attractive qualification for God's prophet and leader. God reveals to Moses his plan for the redemption of Israel from slavery in Egypt and establishing them in a Promised Land and then informs Moses that he, Moses is the one chosen to accomplish this plan. Moses' initial response manifests his quality as a humble man, a quality which the Lord can employ.

> But Moses said to God, 'Who am I that I should go to Pharaoh, and bring the Israelites out of Egypt?'[18]

'Which "I am", which "ego" is going to accomplish this?' asks Moses, aware of his own weakness. God replies, 'I AM will go with you; it is not you, Moses, who will accomplish this thing.' Moses will be the 'God-bearer' because he is humble and has made himself available. It is Moses' very emptiness which appeals to the Lord, for the Lord wants to get into Pharaoh's presence through Moses.

Moses objects a second time out of his humility: 'Then Moses answered, "But suppose they do not believe me or listen to me, but say, 'The Lord did not appear to you.'"'[19]

---

17 Num. 12:3.
18 Exod. 3:11.
19 Exod. 4:1.

Moses has no signs of power – he is a weakling. God clearly likes this about Moses and says in effect: 'You supply the staff, your right arm and a little water; I will add the power'. The staff becomes a serpent, the right arm becomes leprous and the water turns to blood. Moses supplies the little things of his life; God adds the power. What better definition of a Christian sacrament? 'You bring what you have and offer it to me; I will add the power of heaven.'

Moses objects a third time to his own inadequacy:

> But Moses said to the Lord, 'O my Lord, I have never been eloquent, neither in the past or even now that you have spoken to your servant; but I am slow of speech and slow of tongue.'[20]

'And that's the third thing I like about you, Moses,' says the Lord. 'You really don't speak very well! You supply the empty mouth, Moses, and I'll supply the words.[21] Now go to Pharaoh!' In a sense we can say that God needs Moses, his entrée into the palace in which he was raised, and his ability to speak Egyptian to Pharaoh; but he only needs Moses insofar as Moses is empty and available.

This parable of the call of Moses begins with God calling him by name from the burning bush. Moses responds with the very words that are regularly used by the humble servants of God throughout the Scriptures: 'Here I am'; 'Behold! Me'. 'At your service, Lord'. Abraham, Jacob, Moses, Samuel and Mary all employ the formula to offer themselves to God for humble service.

As we have already seen with the sin of the golden calf, the real sin was the peoples' worship out of fear of an item of human manufacture. Moses descends from Sinai without the tablets of the commandments to bring them to repentance. They cannot even receive the Ten Commandments and make a covenant with the Lord until they have turned

20 Exod. 4:10.
21 We are reminded of John's Gospel where, in the first chapter, he states: 'And the word became flesh and dwelt among us'.

from the god of their own making to become humble and empty once more. The purpose of repentance, then, is always to turn from the fundamental sin of self-worship which is signified by idolatry, and a return to self-emptying; repentance is the prerequisite of faith and reception of the law of God. Law-keeping does not replace repentance, for law-keeping can, as some of the Pharisees were told by Jesus, become an idolatry itself. St Paul makes it clear that law-keeping cannot bring salvation.

We have spoken above concerning national prejudice and pride in chosenness and Israel's departure from the humility of the wilderness, especially during the time of the kings. In fact, God's permission for the people to have a king at all is couched in the warning that such an institution represents a clear departure from the faith and humility of the wilderness institutions. The warnings in Deuteronomy already cited above are the conditions for a king which would also maintain the national dependence upon the Lord (Deuteronomy 17:14–20), and we have noted how Solomon contravened each and every point of this legislation. We have also observed that David's psalm in 2 Samuel 22, while it extols humility as over against haughtiness, 'You deliver a humble people, but your eyes are upon the haughty to bring them down,'[22] nevertheless demonstrates very little of that virtue in the rest of the psalm as being a personal trait of David's.

One of the kings of the House of David does offer us a model of repentance when he becomes ill and fears death. This is King Hezekiah:

In those days Hezekiah became sick and was at the point of death. The prophet Isaiah son of Amoz came to him, and said to him, 'Thus says the Lord: Set your house in order, for you shall die; you shall not recover'. Then Hezekiah turned his face to the wall and prayed to the Lord: 'Remember now,

22 2 Sam. 22:28 (Ps. 18:27 'For you deliver a humble people, but the haughty eyes you bring down'). See also Prov. 3:34: 'Toward the scorners he is scornful, but to the humble he shows favour.'

O Lord, I implore you, how I have walked before you in faithfulness with a whole heart, and have done what is good in your sight'. Hezekiah wept bitterly. Before Isaiah had gone out of the middle court, the word of the Lord came to him: 'Turn back, and say to Hezekiah prince of my people, Thus says the Lord, the God of your ancestor David: I have heard your prayer, I have seen your tears; indeed, I will heal you; on the third day you shall go up to the house of the Lord. I will add fifteen years to your life. I will deliver you and this city out of the hand of the king of Assyria; I will defend this city for my own sake and for my servant David's sake'.[23]

The Lord is moved by repentance and tears. It is probably significant that the Lord calls Hezekiah 'the prince of my people' and not 'the king'; 'prince' suggests that the real King is God himself and that the House of David rules only on sufferance of the Almighty. Zechariah, a prophet after the fall of Jerusalem and the exile, foresees this new kind of king for the great messianic festival of the Temple, the Feast of Tabernacles or Booths when the king rides into Jerusalem on the royal mule amidst the hosannas of the people:

Rejoice greatly, O daughter Zion! Shout aloud, O daughter Jerusalem! Lo, your king comes to you; triumphant and victorious is he, humble and riding on a donkey, on a colt, the foal of a donkey. He will cut off the chariot from Ephraim and the war-horse from Jerusalem; and the battle bow shall be cut off, and he shall command peace to the nations; his dominion shall be from sea to sea, and from the River to the ends of the earth. As for you also, because of the blood of my covenant with you, I will set your prisoners free from the waterless pit. Return to your stronghold, O prisoners of hope; today I declare that I will restore to you double.[24]

23 2 Kgs. 20:1–6.
24 Zech. 9:9–12.

The destruction of Jerusalem and its royal family and Judah's time in exile seem to have gone a long way to reversing the national prejudice introduced by the kings. For here we have a vision of the king coming up to the royal city on the great festival of the rains as in days of old, surrounded by the crowds with their willow, laurel and palm branches shouting the hosannas as in former days, but now the king is described as 'humble' and seeking an end to wars and the exercise of power. National repentance in exile has put away national pride and the arrogance of election; thus God relents and allows his people to come home.

We have already suggested at the beginning of chapter two that the parable of Job gives insight into Judah/Jerusalem's later understanding of God's purposes in allowing the exile in Babylon. We must now look at Job from the standpoint of national repentance and humility.

Job, as we have suggested, is the figure of Judah/Jerusalem itself. Job is a righteous man, in fact the most righteous of his generation. He is scrupulous about making sacrifices, not only for himself but also for his children. God holds Job up to the Satan as a model of righteousness,[25] and the Satan makes the observation: 'Yes, but he can afford to be righteous; you've given him everything. Take away his wealth and family and see how righteous he is.' The Lord replies: 'Try it'. The parable continues with the dispossession of Job, just as Jerusalem was reduced in wealth and power even before the coming of Nebuchadnezzar. Yet Job remains faithful, even in the misfortunes of loss, and does not blame God for the disaster.

The Lord holds Job up to the Satan a second time as still righteous, and the Satan replies: 'He still has his health and his skin. Touch that and he won't be so righteous.' The Lord says: 'Do it'. Thus Job's very body is destroyed and he

---

25 The Satan in Job is a functionary of the divine court and is the attorney general of the Kingdom of God, wandering through it from end to end to keep the order of the kingdom. The tribulations of Job are not the Satan's doing but God's.

is left in dust and ashes, just as the wall of Jerusalem is breached and the city left in ruins. But Job is not moved to blame God for being unrighteous.

Finally we are given the vision of Job's demise and the taunts under the guise of comfort from his three friends, the wise men from the east. They taunt Job with the 'wisdom' of the world: 'Job, real wisdom holds that the righteous are rewarded and the unrighteous are punished; surely, that is the way of the Lord. Now if you are being punished, then it follows that you have been unrighteous!' Job is finally pushed to despair: 'I am righteous and my punishment is unfair and unjust. Since it is God that is punishing me, it follows that God himself is unjust and unfair.'

For chapter after chapter Job protests his innocence and his righteousness; and for chapter after chapter Job sinks lower and lower in the pit he is digging for himself by charging God with unrighteousness and unfairness. So too must the people of Judah and Jerusalem now in exile in Babylon have protested their righteousness as the 'chosen people' and accused God of unfairness as they behold the destruction of the holy city and the Temple. The charge that God is unrighteous is the ultimate arrogance. We have only to remember God's sensitivity on this point in the argument of Abraham over the Lord's plan to destroy the wicked city of Sodom:

> Far be it from you to do such a thing, to slay the righteous with the wicked, so that the righteous fare as the wicked! Far be that from you! Shall not the Judge of all the earth do what is just?[26]

The Lord finally agrees with Abraham that he would spare the city if only ten righteous folk are found there, so keen is the Lord concerning his righteousness and so patient is he in waiting for repentance.

Thus Job continues to offend the Almighty by his arro-

26 Gen. 18:25.

gance that what has happened to him is not fair. Finally the Lord has enough of Job's protestations and confronts Job in the whirlwind of power with the creation itself, calling on Job to match his feeble sense of what is fair and just with the creation by God of Justice and Fairness itself in the way that the universe works.

> Then the Lord answered Job out of the whirlwind: 'Who is this that darkens counsel by words without knowledge? Gird up your loins like a man, I will question you, and you shall declare to me. Where were you when I laid the foundation of the earth? Tell me, if you have understanding.'[27]

Again, for chapter after chapter the Lord turns the knife in Job's arrogance until finally Job cries out, 'Enough!'

> Then Job answered the Lord: 'I know that you can do all things, and that no purpose of yours can be thwarted. "Who is this that hides counsel without knowledge?" Therefore I have uttered what I did not understand, things too wonderful for me, which I did not know. "Hear, and I will speak; I will question you, and you declare to me." I had heard of you by the hearing of the ear, but now my eye sees you; therefore I despise myself, and repent in dust and ashes.'[28]

The operative word in Job's response to the Lord's anger is, of course, 'I repent in dust and ashes'. And no sooner does Job repent than the Lord refers to him again as 'My servant Job'. He then reveals to Job what his affliction means. For he addresses Job's three friends, the 'wise' men from the east:

> After the Lord had spoken these words to Job, the Lord said to Eliphaz the Temanite: 'My wrath is kindled against you and against your two friends; for you have not spoken of me what is right, as my servant Job has. Now therefore take seven bulls and seven rams, and go to my servant Job, and

27 Job 38:1–4.
28 Job 42:1–6.

offer up for yourselves a burnt offering; and my servant Job shall pray for you, for I will accept his prayer not to deal with you according to your folly; for you have not spoken of me what is right, as my servant Job has done.'[29]

Why has Job, the servant of God suffered? Why has he become the suffering servant? In order to save the three friends from the wrath of God! God rewards Job by saving his friends – who, like the three wise men in Matthew's Gospel, represent the nations of the earth. But Job, like Jonah, cannot engage in mission until his humility is restored, until he himself repents.

Why have Judah and Jerusalem gone into exile? The answer of the Book of Job is: 'To save Babylon!' It is as though the Lord is saying to his people, 'Israel, you are my elect; but I have chosen you to accomplish my purposes, the mission for which I have called you. If you glory in your election but do not carry out the mission I have set for you, I will have to purify you of your pride and restore your humility so that you may be once more a useful vessel and a servant.'

Israel's humility and simple dependence on God is most clearly to be seen in the Wilderness experience. Psalm 81 recalls these early times with God from the depths of the exile in Babylon:

> Give ear, O Shepherd of Israel, you who lead Joseph like a flock! You who are enthroned upon the cherubim, shine forth before Ephraim and Benjamin and Manasseh. Stir up your might, and come to save us! Restore us, O God; let your face shine, that we may be saved. O Lord God of hosts, how long will you be angry with your people's prayers? You have fed them with the bread of tears, and given them tears to drink in full measure. You make us the scorn of our neighbours; our enemies laugh among themselves. Restore us, O God of hosts; let your face shine, that we may be saved. You brought a vine out of Egypt; you drove out the nations and planted it. You

---

29 Job 42:7–8.

cleared the ground for it; it took deep root and filled the land. The mountains were covered with its shade, the mighty cedars with its branches; it sent out its branches to the sea, and its shoots to the River. Why then have you broken down its walls, so that all who pass along the way pluck its fruit? The boar from the forest ravages it, and all that move in the field feed on it. Turn again, O God of hosts; look down from heaven, and see; have regard for this vine, the stock that your right hand planted. They have burned it with fire, they have cut it down; may they perish at the rebuke of your countenance. But let your hand be upon the one at your right hand, the one whom you made strong for yourself. Then we will never turn back from you; give us life, and we will call on your name. Restore us, O Lord God of hosts; let your face shine, that we may be saved.

Another psalm defines wickedness as the opposite of humility and reminds us of God's general rule to all humankind which he gives first to Cain before he murders his brother: 'If you do the Good, will you not be accepted? And if you do not do the Good, sin is lurking at the door; its desire is for you, but you must master it.'[30] The psalm is Psalm 36:

Transgression speaks to the wicked deep in their hearts; there is no fear of God before their eyes. For they flatter themselves in their own eyes that their iniquity cannot be found out and hated. The words of their mouths are mischief and deceit; they have ceased to act wisely and do the good. They plot mischief while on their beds; they are set on a way that is not good; they do not reject evil.

This 'fear of the Lord', which is really humility, is a consistent theme throughout Scripture. It is that great virtue which captures God's attention, just as he is moved by the repentance that restores humility:

The prayer of the humble pierces the clouds, and it will not rest until it reaches its goal; it will not desist until the Most

30 Gen. 4:7.

High responds and does justice for the righteous, and executes judgement.[31]

The prelude to the New Testament, the Magnificat of Mary, reiterates the pre-eminence of humility:

He has shown strength with his arm; he has scattered the proud in the thoughts of their hearts. He has brought down the powerful from their thrones, and lifted up the lowly; he has filled the hungry with good things, and sent the rich away empty. He has helped his servant Israel, in remembrance of his mercy, according to the promise he made to our ancestors, to Abraham and to his descendants forever.[32]

The very life of Jesus in the Gospels is a life based upon humility; the preachment of Jesus is grounded in his saying: 'Take my yoke upon you, and learn from me; for I am gentle and humble in heart, and you will find rest for your souls'.[33] The temptations of the wilderness are all temptations against humility – 'Serve yourself', says the Satan. 'I will only serve the Lord', replies Jesus. Even when Jesus, in affirmation of his Davidic kingship, rides into Jerusalem on the great royal feast of Tabernacles[34] on the donkey, the Judean king's beast, he does so with none of the power, glory and arrogance of a David or a Solomon, but in accordance with the prophet Zechariah's vision of the way it must be when Israel is restored to its patrimony:

Tell the daughter of Zion, 'Look, your king is coming to you, humble, and mounted on a donkey, and on a colt, the foal of a donkey.'[35]

31 Sir. 35:21–2.
32 Luke 1:51–5.
33 Matt. 11:29.
34 We call it Palm Sunday, but in fact it is the Jerusalemite and Temple Feast of Tabernacles or Succoth; cf. my article 'Palm Sunday; the Christian Feast of Tabernacles' in *Christian News from Israel (new series)*, Vol. 24, No. 1, pp. 16–24 (Ministry of Religious Affairs, Jerusalem: Summer, 1973).
35 Matt. 21:5‖Zech. 9:9.

Perhaps the most beautiful and powerful declaration of the humility of Jesus is to be found in St Paul's great Hymn of the Kenosis[36] of Jesus:

> Do nothing from selfish ambition or conceit, but in humility regard others as better than yourselves. Let each of you look not to your own interests, but to the interests of others. Let the same mind be in you that was in Christ Jesus, who, though he was in the form of God, did not regard equality with God as something to be exploited, but emptied himself, taking the form of a slave, being born in human likeness. And being found in human form, he humbled himself and became obedient to the point of death – even death on a cross. Therefore God also highly exalted him and gave him the name that is above every name, so that at the name of Jesus every knee should bend, in heaven and on earth and under the earth, and every tongue should confess that Jesus Christ is Lord, to the glory of God the Father.[37]

How different is this humility from the military arrogance of a Constantine or the ecclesiastical arrogance of a Borgia pope! Better is the agenda of humility which the Lord gives in his Sermon on the Mount:

> Blessed are the poor in spirit, for theirs is the kingdom of heaven. Blessed are those who mourn, for they will be comforted. Blessed are the meek, for they will inherit the earth. Blessed are those who hunger and thirst for righteousness, for they will be filled. Blessed are the merciful, for they will receive mercy. Blessed are the pure in heart, for they will see God. Blessed are the peacemakers, for they will be called children of God. Blessed are those who are persecuted for righteousness' sake, for theirs is the kingdom of heaven. Blessed are you when people revile you and persecute you and utter all kinds of evil against you falsely on my account. Rejoice and be glad, for your reward is great in heaven, for in the same way they persecuted the prophets who were before you.[38]

36 or 'self-emptying' of Jesus.
37 Phil. 2:3–11.
38 Matt. 5:3–12.

While these beatitudes seem like a counsel for weakness, even failure, they are in fact a digest of the way of the humility so beloved of God. They remind us of the Evangelical Counsels, poverty, chastity and obedience, which are yet another statement of the virtue of humility.

The power of humility, seemingly a contradiction in terms, may also be seen at work in the secular world in the Satyagraha, or non-violent resistance of Mohandas Gandhi in his struggle for Indian independence and his opposition to apartheid in South Africa. Martin Luther King employed this tool of humility in the Civil Rights Movement in the United States.

Returning to Jonah, when the people of Nineveh believed God, they immediately repented and signified their humility in that 'they proclaimed a fast, and everyone, great and small, put on sackcloth', levelling the great and small in their humble stance before the Lord.

III. 6 *When the news reached the king of Nineveh, he rose from his throne, removed his robe, covered himself with sackcloth, and sat in ashes.*

In the ancient Near East there was, of course, no notion of the modern nation state in which the ruler and the ruled are separate from each other and can be studied or understood separately. There were no constitutional monarchs, no democracy, and no executive branch. Rather, king and people were of a piece, father and sons. What the king did, the people did. Only the relationship between the king and the deity tended to differ somewhat. For example, in Egypt king and deity coalesced; when the king spoke, his word was the word of deity itself.[39] Nor was the king in Egypt in

---

39 We get a sense of these relationships and Pharaoh's authority in the story of Joseph: 'And Pharaoh said to Joseph, "You shall be over my house, and all my people shall order themselves as you command; only with regard to the throne will I be greater than you." Moreover Pharaoh said to Joseph, "I am Pharaoh, and without your Word no one shall lift up hand or foot in all the land of Egypt."' Gen. 41:40, 44.

any way bound by the law, for he gave the law which was interpreted by the wise men and promulgated by them to the kingdom. Deity and the pharaoh were one and the peoples totally dependent on Pharaoh for their life and well-being. The pyramid is an excellent symbol of kingship and people in Egypt; the capstone at the top and alone in the heavens is pharaonic deity itself and the remainder of the structure anonymous stones supporting the top.

In Mesopotamia, while the relationship of king and people is still a unity, the relationship of king and deity is somewhat different from that in Egypt. King and deity do not coalesce and the king is subject to deity and receives the laws from deity, as Hammurabi received his Code from the deity Shamash. The king is bound by the law in the same way that his people are.[40]

It is, perhaps, also useful in this context to think of the relationship of a flock to its shepherd, for the good king to his people is like a good shepherd vis-à-vis his flock; the bad shepherd, or hireling, cares nothing for the flock and will leave them wanting 'as sheep without a shepherd'.

In the parable of Jonah we are not told the relationship of the king with the deities of Assyria. But we are to understand that when the king of Nineveh abandons his two signs of power and authority, his throne and his royal vestments, it is a sign not only of his own abdication in favour of God as king but that all of his people, indicated here by 'his nobles' are one with him in this great act of repentance. Thus we hear of the repentance of the whole people, a people who are Israel's persecutors and its arch-enemy!

The king's abandonment of his throne as abdication is followed by his stripping off his robes of state, the very sign of his royal glory.[41] Sackcloth is the traditional garb for a

40 This is reminiscent of Moses receiving the Law on Sinai from God. Solomon, on the other hand, was the Law incarnate and his Word went out from Jerusalem and ordered the whole land – more on the Egyptian model.

41 See again Gen. 41 for the vesting of Joseph with the power of the royal adornments. Notice too the description of the adornments of

mourner and replaces the robes of state. Dust and ashes are the sign of humility, service and the self-emptying of repentance. Psalm 101 describes the liturgy of the deposition of the king in favour of the King of all the earth:

> The nations will fear the name of the Lord, and all the kings of the earth your glory. For the Lord will build up Zion; he will appear in his glory. He will regard the prayer of the destitute (הָעַרְעָר = 'stripped'), and will not despise their prayer.[42]

Like Job, the king of Nineveh 'repented in dust and ashes', and with him the entire people. We may well wonder why the king of the world power which was Nineveh might even consider repentance. Could he have been afraid of something? While it can only be speculation of the most general order, it seems possible that while the King of Assyria, Sargon II, at the time of the destruction of the Kingdom of Israel in 721 BCE certainly had little to fear in the way of any powerful opposition, yet the later king of that nation, Ashur-etil-ilani, had a great deal to fear from the new powers, the Medes and the Babylonians, before Nineveh was in its turn destroyed and razed to the ground in 612 BCE. Weakness and failure arouse the kind of fear of the storm that befell the captain and his crew in chapter one of this parable.

Of course, every encounter with God and every conversion is ultimately a mystery. But whatever the motive of the king of Nineveh's repentance, it is clear that it certainly would not have happened without Jonah's carrying the Word of God to Nineveh.

---

the High Priest described in Exodus and in Sirach 50 (quoted earlier). The High Priest cannot make the sacrifice on the Day of Atonement without the vestments and crown, and in Jesus' day, these special robes were locked up in the Roman fortress, the Antonia, and issued to the High Priest only with the permission of the Procurator to emphasize the power of Rome over high-priestly authority.

42 Ps. 102:15–17.

The Word of God is powerful, as it says:

> The law of the Lord is perfect, reviving the soul; the decrees
> of the Lord are sure, making wise the simple; the precepts of
> the Lord are right, rejoicing the heart; the commandment of
> the Lord is clear, enlightening the eyes; the fear of the Lord
> is pure, enduring forever; the ordinances of the Lord are true
> and righteous altogether. More to be desired are they than
> gold, even much fine gold; sweeter also than honey, and
> drippings of the honeycomb.[43]

Yet St Paul knows the truth about the mission of the
prophet and those chosen by the Lord to be his messengers:

> But how are they to call on one in whom they have not
> believed? And how are they to believe in one of whom they
> have never heard? And how are they to hear without
> someone to proclaim him? And how are they to proclaim
> him unless they are sent? As it is written, 'How beautiful are
> the feet of those who bring good news!'[44]

III. 7 *And he made proclamation and published through Nineveh, to wit: 'By the decree of the king and his nobles: Let neither man nor beast, herd nor flock, taste anything; let them not feed, or drink water,*

A fast is here the sign of 'self-emptying', of repentance
leading to humility. The king and his council of wise men
extend their own self-deposition, quite naturally, to the
people over whom they rule. But more; it is not an edict for
the people alone, but for the flocks and herds which they
own. What the king does, the people do; and what the
people do, the living things over which the people have
jurisdiction do as well. In short, the whole land is to repent.

---

43 Ps. 19:7–10.
44 Rom. 10:14–15.

We are reminded of the jurisdiction which Adam[45] is given over all other living things at the time of Adam's creation. As the people are related to the king as his dependents, so the creatures are related to the people as dependents. In the parable, the 'city of Nineveh' means all living things in Nineveh.

We must remember here the fast of Jesus in the wilderness for forty days, after which he is able to reply to the Tempter's suggestion about food, 'Man does not live by bread alone, but by every Word that comes from the mouth of God'.[46] Apparently the emptiness which comes of fasting makes one more susceptible to hearing the Word of God:

> And he [Moses] was there with the Lord forty days and forty nights; he neither ate bread nor drank water. And he wrote upon the tables the words of the covenant, the Ten Commandments.[47]

Only with a fast from the nourishments of this earth can we enjoy what is promised in Psalm 23:

> He makes me lie down in green pastures; he leads me beside still waters; he restores my soul. He leads me in right paths for his name's sake ... You prepare a table before me in the presence of my enemies; you anoint my head with oil; my cup overflows.[48]

45 It is useful to recall that 'adam' in Hebrew always means 'human being' as distinct from all other 'critters'; adam does not mean 'man' as opposed to 'woman'. The feminine form of adam, that is ad'mah, means the dust of the earth from which adam was taken and to which adam will return. The name is a word-play and pun. To know this is to be spared much distress over political correctness.

46 Deut. 8:3 ‖ Matt. 4:4 ‖ Luke 4:4. See also the feeding of the 5,000, where Jesus is given five loaves, perhaps the five Books of Moses or Torah, and two fish, perhaps the Book of the Prophets and the Book of the Writings. He multiplies them, or preaches on them, and feeds not only the multitude with the Word of God, but has enough (12 baskets) left over to feed all Israel (12 Tribes).

47 Exod. 34:28.

48 Ps. 23:2–3, 5.

III. 8 *Human beings and animals shall be covered with sackcloth, and they shall cry mightily to God. All shall turn from their evil ways and from the violence that is in their hands.*

As with Adam, so with the creatures over which he rules; as with the king, so with his entire kingdom, including all domesticated animals. The intention here is the repentance of all living things in the kingdom, just as God's goal is the repentance of all that lives in the world. In short, God wants his world back. The depth of repentance is to be profound – deepest mourning and penance:

> I will turn your feasts into mourning, and all your songs into lamentation; I will bring sackcloth on all loins, and baldness on every head; I will make it like the mourning for an only son, and the end of it like a bitter day.[49]

The universality of mourning and repentance as a substitute for sacrifices and offerings is a feature of the exile in Babylon and signal Israel's understanding that the Lord is moved only by expressions of humility rather than offering, as there is nothing he does not already possess as the Creator of all save the free decision of humankind to worship him as God. Thus we read:

> They and their wives and their children and their cattle and every resident alien and hired labourer and purchased slave – they all put sackcloth around their waists.

> [Judith] set up a tent for herself on the roof of her house. She put sackcloth around her waist and dressed in widow's clothing.

> Bind on sackcloth and cloth of goats' hair, and wail for your children, and lament for them; for your destruction is at hand.[50]

49 Amos 8:10.
50 Judith 4:10; 8:54; 2 Esdras 16:2.

Sackcloth and the profound mourning for destruction and death go together, as do sackcloth and the traditional 'hair shirt' of the penitent. The colour of sackcloth seems to have been black like the ashes that often accompanied it.

> When he opened the sixth seal, I looked, and there came a great earthquake; the sun became black as sackcloth, the full moon became like blood.[51]

The 'evil ways' from which humankind is to turn in repentance are parallel to 'the violence in their hands' and remind us of the generation of the Flood in the time of Noah, when 'every inclination of man's heart was continuously evil'. We must understand that active sinning is a matter of choice, and that an alternate choice is always possible – thus repentance is not so much of 'getting rid of' something so much as turning from one way to another. It is a decision to turn from a self-centred way of doing things to a God-centred way of doing things. The ancient rabbis and the Dead Sea Covenanters before them described this as 'The Two Inclinations', the inclination to evil and the inclination to the good. The Good is understood to be the same choices of working with God's creative plan first revealed in the parable of creation itself: maintain the boundaries among all things; discern the value of each thing, signified by its name; maintain the balance between and among the parts (defined as 'love' between humans); and preserve and encourage life in every case. To choose the Good results in God's favour, as he said to Cain, 'If you do the Good, you are always acceptable to me'. To choose the other way, to follow the inclination to evil and to serve the self as god and run contrary to the principles of the Good, is called 'sin' and leads to the return of the primeval chaos and death.

Repentance, signed by sackcloth and mourning, indicates a decision to change from following the inclination to evil to the inclination towards the Good. The descent into

51 Rev. 6:12.

repentance reaches the depth which is humility and signals the ascent to a new way in which arrogance and self-centred pride are forsworn and the penitent can say: 'Not my will, but thine be done'.

III. 9 *Who knows? God may relent and change his mind; he may turn from his fierce anger, so that we do not perish.'*

Like the captain of Jonah's ship, the king reminds us of the uncertainty of the mercy of God. The world of the judge and the world of the accused are radically different when it comes to the mercy of the court. While I may know the rules of righteousness which have been revealed to me by authority, and while I may choose to follow or not to follow these laws, to act righteously and justly or to transgress and sin, the matter of whether the judge will exercise mercy in relieving me of punishment for my transgression is completely out of my ken and has nothing to do with my ability to choose. Nor can I offer the judge a bribe to show mercy; I have, in fact, nothing to offer except my profound sorrow for having made the wrong choice and my promise of amendment in the future. And if this is true for a human judge, a judge of flesh and blood, how much more for the Judge of all the earth! Who knows how the judge will respond to my begging for mercy? It is totally a matter of the judge's mind – and heart.

God's repentance and change of mind and heart are completely different from my repentance, though both involve 'turning'. I turn from my choice of following my own inclination to following God's ways, the Good. God's two inclinations, also a matter of choice, are between his inclination towards justice and righteousness by which the very world is sustained and without which the world would fall down and his inclination towards mercy, an exception to justice which in fact perverts the way of righteousness by not following through to the punishment which inevitably lies at the conclusion of every conviction for law-breaking.

When I beg for mercy, I am asking the Creator for an exception to the normal workings of his own universe. I am begging for a miracle. And if he repents from carrying out the sentence to its conclusion of punishment, it is indeed the greatest of miracles.

It would be tempting to think that God's repentance from righteousness to mercy will follow in tandem with my own repentance from my evil ways to my choice of the Good. This, however, would be a mistake; if this were so, I would 'force' God's repentance by my own and I could mechanistically 'win' God's mercy by my own doing.

We are reminded here that God's anger[52] is 'fierce' and that the only real price of restoring the order of creation would be my own death, a price I cannot pay and continue to live. In short, my repentance, while powerful in God's eyes, is not quite enough. There is still the outstanding debt of the damage my 'violence' has caused God's majesty.

Once again we are reminded of the 'sign of Jonah', the innocent whose invitation to the sinners is: 'Take me, bind me and throw me overboard'. While normal sacrifices and offerings would, if used in this case, constitute only a bribe, there is one sacrifice which is acceptable, yes, even needful. The formula is that of the High Priest of Israel on the Day of Atonement as established by Aaron's brother Moses at the Sin of the Golden Calf: 'If you will forgive them, please forgive them [for they were afraid and didn't know what they were doing]; but if not, take my life instead of theirs.'

This interplay between repentance and the atonement sacrifice is beautifully described in John's Gospel in John's first 'sign' or witness to the cross.[53] Before the parable of the wedding feast at Cana, we find John the Baptist baptizing for repentance in the River Jordan; the narrative continues with the appearance of Jesus and John's identification of him as 'the Lamb of God', that is, the atonement sacri-

---

52 God's anger is graphically described in Hebrew as 'His nose turning flaming red'.
53 John 2:1–11.

fice which will complete what has begun with the repentance of baptism. The work of repentance is not finished without the subsequent atonement sacrifice.

The wedding feast at Cana and its conclusion are the parable which demonstrates this 'finishing' of the 'turning' of God from justice to mercy. Cana is, at best, an insignificant and tiny burg, in keeping with God's preference for the little and humble. There is a wedding there to which Jesus, his mother and his disciples have come.

It is crucial to the story at this point to know that a wedding in Israel must include wine, for wine is the 'rejoicing of the heart' which is the sign of the life-giving nature of a wedding. There can be no wedding without wine, just as there can be no Mass without wine. And we are told, 'The wine runs out'; the wedding cannot proceed.

The dialogue of Mary with her son, here as everywhere in the Gospels, represents the movement from the mundane to the heavenly.[54] She calls to Jesus' attention that there is a social disaster. His response raises the parable to a heavenly plane: 'Mother, your concerns are not mine; my hour has not yet come'. In short, this is not an insignificant matter of this tiny wedding; this has to do with Jesus' entire purpose in the world

Then we come to the nature of the real wedding which is intended here. There are, standing in the tiny house, six stone water jars for the rites of purification, each holding some thirty gallons – each! Now here is a wondrous thing. Why would a tiny house in an insignificant village have six enormous jars for purification rites? And, more importantly, why are they empty? Perhaps there has not been the purification which should have preceded the wedding.

The mystery is partially solved if we think of another wedding, that is, the renewal of the marriage contract, or covenant, between God and his people in the Temple on the great Feast of Tabernacles. In fact, all individual weddings

---

54 See also Matt. 12:46–50 ‖ Mk. 3:31–5 ‖ Lk. 8:19–21; Lk. 2:43–50; Lk. 14:26; Jn 19:25–7.

in Israel are reminders of the big wedding between God and his people/bride, the anniversary of which is annually celebrated by the Tabernacles festival on the fifteenth day of the seventh month (the autumn) at the Temple. In the Temple are located the great jars for the water of purification which are a feature of the Day of Atonement, Yom Kippur, five days before Tabernacles. The rites of purification must precede the wedding. We can only wonder why the jars are empty; perhaps the Temple purification rites were a matter of emptiness, voided maybe by the irregularity of the Temple priesthood and the 'paganization' and 'hellenization' of the priestly family in Jesus' day. Certainly this family was in no way connected to the priesthood of either Aaron or Zadok, and was more concerned with keeping the Romans from destroying the Temple than with the relationship with God.

In any event, Jesus, the true High Priest of Aaron, demands that the jars be filled with water, presumably to re-inaugurate the rites of purification. Immediately, the water turns to wine and the wedding can go on. Clearly, the steward of the feast, the reigning High Priest, does not know where the wine has come from, especially since it is the finest wine. Only one mystery remains: there should be seven water jars rather than only six. Repentance and purification are not quite enough; something further remains.

The solution to John's mystery occurs at the seventh sign, the crucifixion of Jesus, the sacrifice of the High Priest.

> When the soldiers had crucified Jesus, they took his clothes and divided them into four parts, one for each soldier.[55] They also took his tunic; now the tunic was seamless, woven in one piece from the top. So they said to one another, 'Let us not tear it, but cast lots for it to see who will get it'. This was to fulfill what the scripture says, 'They divided my

---

55 Clearly, John wants us to think of the four corners of the earth; these soldiers, like the sailors on Jonah's boat, are from every nation under heaven. The sacrifice is for them.

clothes among themselves, and for my clothing they cast lots'. And that is what the soldiers did. Meanwhile, standing near the cross of Jesus were his mother, and his mother's sister, Mary the wife of Clopas, and Mary Magdalene. When Jesus saw his mother and the disciple whom he loved standing beside her, he said to his mother, 'Woman, here is your son'. Then he said to the disciple, 'Here is your mother'. And from that hour the disciple took her into his own home. After this, when Jesus knew that all was now finished, he said (in order to fulfill the scripture), 'I am thirsty'. A jar full of sour wine was standing there. So they put a sponge full of the wine on a branch of hyssop and held it to his mouth. When Jesus had received the wine, he said, 'It is finished'. Then he bowed his head and gave up his spirit.[56]

Jesus, the High Priest, is wearing the seamless undergarment which is the vestment of the High Priest on the Day of Atonement. Lots are cast to determine the Lamb of God. Mary reappears to hear that filial piety must be replaced by the great sacrifice of the Son. Then Jesus thirsts. And at the foot of the cross, the altar of the atonement sacrifice, stands the missing seventh stone water jar, now full of almost-finished (raw, not vinegar) wine. They put it to his lips on the rod, which reminds us of the first sinner, Cain (whose name means 'reed'), and Jesus cries out: 'It is consummated';[57] the great Wedding between God and his people

---

56 John 19:23–30.
57 The verb 'to finish' in the Hebrew, when used about creation and all the other dwelling places of God in Scripture, has a technical meaning indicating the place of the Lord's coming to earth – the incarnation. As with creation, the Tabernacle/Temples always take seven (days or years) to set up. This includes the Tabernacle in the wilderness, Solomon's Temple, the second Temple after the exile and here, where Jesus has declared that he would set up the new Temple of his body in three days (but after the seven signs that John recounts during his ministry). Because the creation and the Temples are the 'containers' of God's glorious presence, the verb 'to finish' and the word for 'vessel' are related to each other.
Following the imagery of the bride welcoming the bridegroom into

can proceed to consummation for the outstanding price has been made with his sacrifice. Repentance and purification plus the atonement sacrifice brings the mercy of God for all who repent and then catch hold of the binding over of this Sacrifice, Jesus, the great High Priest, who gives his life now for the world.[58] God has indeed relented and changed his mind so that the world will not perish.

III. 10 *When God saw what they did, how they turned from their evil ways, God changed his mind about the calamity that he had said he would bring upon them; and he did not do it.*

The repentance of the king and people of Nineveh has indeed moved the Lord to show mercy rather than to carry out the sentence of calamity and death which he had pronounced upon them. This willingness of God to change his mind is never to be confused with the capriciousness of the deities of the world, for mercy is always costly in that it involves the sacrifice and abandonment of that which is most precious to the Lord, namely his justice and right-

---

her, she becomes the vessel; so the word for 'vessel' and the word for 'bride' are related in Hebrew. Thus when Jesus says, 'It is finished' or 'it is consummated', the imagery is all of a piece. In modern Judaism, the Sabbath is often called the 'Sabbath Bride' in that God comes together with his people at this special time as was especially the case on the Feast of Tabernacles in Temple times. Jewish weddings feature bride and groom standing under the *chuppah*, a small bower bedecked with flowers and representing the Temple of old where the annual wedding anniversary celebrations were held between God and his people. Careful examination will show that the covenants God makes with Israel are – all of them – marriage contracts. The Church uses the same imagery with Jesus as the bridegroom and the Church as his bride. The symbolism of the great Liturgy of the Easter Vigil when the paschal candle, the light of Christ, is plunged three times into the waters of the womb of the Church, the baptismal font, leaves little to the imagination, especially when God, like any father, wants children. But then sex in Scripture is most holy rather than polluted.

58 John 3:16.

eousness. It can only be understood as the profound 'weakness' and 'humility' of the Lord in his passion for the Adam which he has made. It is God's Weakness and Passion which confounds all reasonable and rational theology[59] and puts the Lord God well beyond the realms of human knowing or understanding. It is a Love we cannot know but only experience in our own weakness and humility.

59 Perhaps the poetic theology of a George Herbert or a John Donne – and though hardly an Anglican Divine, the theology of Hans Urs von Balthazar – comes closer to this non-rational theology. A comparison of these Anglican Divines with the likes of St Thomas Aquinas would perhaps give the flavour of the difference.

Chapter Four

We have seen that repentance is not enough to move God to his own turning from justice to mercy. The liturgy of salvation requires also the sacrifice of the spotless lamb, the atonement. The parable of Jonah moves back now from the king and the people of Nineveh and their repentance to Jonah himself, much as the parable of the salvation of the captain and sailors from the hell of the storm in chapter one moves to dealing with the sacrifice of Jonah and the dynamics of the descent into hell in chapter two.

We should be able to say at the end of chapter three, 'All's well that ends well'; there should be no need for this chapter. But our parable is entitled 'The Reluctant Missionary' and the sacrifice by Jonah of his own passion for justice and 'fairness' for himself. Once more we are reminded that Jonah and Israel are of a piece, and the reluctance of Jonah is really the reluctance of God's people to move beyond their comfortable self-indulgent 'chosenness' to the task for which they were chosen in the first place, the task of mission.

Nineveh's repentance and salvation come as terrible blows to the chosen ones; if, as Job's friends are so keen to tell him repeatedly, 'the good are rewarded and the bad

punished', then Nineveh should in all justice be punished
severely by a just God. God's way of mercy for the enemies
of his people infuriates both Job and Jonah to the point of
wishing for death rather than living with a God who is so
manifestly unjust.

IV. 1 *But it displeased Jonah exceedingly, and he was angry.*

It is the way of children to wish to be the centre of parental
attention and affection. When a child is frustrated in this
desire for attention, it sulks and becomes angry sometimes
to the point of fury, kicking out in every direction. Such was
the case with the first children, the twin boys Cain and
Abel, sons of humankind, of Adam and Eve. Driven to
discover which of them God loved the most, they engaged
in a sacrificing contest of their own devising and invention.
Somehow they decided that Cain 'lost' and Abel 'won'.
Cain, the loser, is displeased and becomes jealous. Though
warned by God of the end of such jealousy, his anger gets
the better of him and he is moved to murder so that he can
obtain the favour from God which he 'deserves' and so that
he can take revenge on his brother.

That the Lord shows mercy to Nineveh is confused by
Jonah with favouritism to Nineveh over Israel; and Jonah is
profoundly jealous and angry. It is clearly not fair that God
should behave in this way and abandon his people in favour
of sinners. Such jealousy has marked the relationships
among peoples and nations from the beginning. The jealousy of the Church directed at the Jewish people, bringing
pogroms and autos-da-fe in its train, is no different in
motive from that which drives Jonah at this point. And it is
significant that we read in the Gospel Pontius Pilate's own
evaluation of the trial of Jesus: 'For he perceived that for
jealousy the chief priests had delivered him up'.[1]

1 Mark 15:10.

This jealousy of the chosen for the recently repented and the mercies that are offered the apparently unworthy are the subject of Jesus' parable of the Prodigal Son's older brother:

> Now his elder son was in the field; and when he came and approached the house, he heard music and dancing. He called one of the slaves and asked what was going on. He replied, 'Your brother has come, and your father has killed the fatted calf, because he has got him back safe and sound'. Then he became angry and refused to go in. His father came out and began to plead with him. But he answered his father, 'Listen! For all these years I have been working like a slave for you, and I have never disobeyed your command; yet you have never given me even a young goat so that I might celebrate with my friends. But when this son of yours came back, who has devoured your property with prostitutes, you killed the fatted calf for him!' Then the father said to him, 'Son, you are always with me, and all that is mine is yours. But we had to celebrate and rejoice, because this brother of yours was dead and has come to life; he was lost and has been found'.[2]

This older brother, so faithful to the father and so angry with the father's merciful reception of his wastrel brother, is clearly identical with our Jonah's state of mind at this point.

IV. 2 *He prayed to the Lord and said, 'O Lord! Is not this what I said while I was still in my own country? That is why I fled to Tarshish at the beginning; for I knew that you are a gracious God and merciful, slow to anger, and abounding in steadfast love, and ready to relent from punishing.*

This prayer of Jonah's is in no way a pious utterance on Jonah's part but a petulant whine. Jonah reveals his real reason for running away from home to Tarshish in the very

---

2 Luke 15:25–32.

beginning of the parable. Jonah knows God so well that he knew why God was sending him to Nineveh and exactly what would be the outcome of his preachment to that wicked city. We might translate this as: 'I know what you're like, and I just knew you would end up saving these wicked folks; and they don't deserve to be saved! you're such a sucker for repentance.'

Jonah knows God because he knows the Lord's real name. God's Name is first revealed to Moses following the sin of the golden calf, the repentance of the people and the establishment of the high priesthood under Aaron. When God finally agrees to go in person with Israel through the wilderness, Moses asks the Lord to show him his face. God demurs about the face but promises his Name instead.

> The Lord said to Moses, 'I will do the very thing that you have asked; for you have found favour in my sight, and I know you by name'. Moses said, 'Show me your glory, I pray'. And he said, 'I will make all my goodness pass before you, and will proclaim before you the name, "The LORD"; and I will be gracious to whom I will be gracious, and will show mercy on whom I will show mercy. But,' he said, 'you cannot see my face; for no one shall see me and live.' And the Lord continued, 'See, there is a place by me where you shall stand on the rock; and while my glory passes by I will put you in a cleft of the rock, and I will cover you with my hand until I have passed by; then I will take away my hand, and you shall see my back; but my face shall not be seen.'[3]

> The Lord descended in the cloud and stood with him there, and proclaimed the name, 'The LORD'. The Lord passed before him, and proclaimed, 'The LORD, the LORD, a God merciful and gracious, slow to anger, and abounding in steadfast love and faithfulness, keeping steadfast love for the thousandth generation, forgiving iniquity and transgression and sin, yet by no means clearing the guilty, but visiting the iniquity of the parents upon the children and the children's

3 Exod. 33:17–23.

children, to the third and the fourth generation.' And Moses
quickly bowed his head toward the earth, and worshipped.[4]

Like the pharaohs of Egypt, the Lord's Name is a compound
of behavioural attributes rather than a modern-type name of
essential 'being'. The attempt to relate 'YHWH' to some form
of the verb 'to be' because of the pun which God plays earlier
in Exodus on Moses' terrified question 'Which "I" are you
talking about going to Egypt to confront Pharaoh?' and the
Lord's response, 'I am [going to Egypt – your 'I' is taking me
there]' is a meaningless speculation on God's Name. His real
Name is how he behaves, a description of his two 'inclinations' to justice and to mercy, which Name is frequently
invoked in the biblical narrative. When Jonah says, 'I know
you' he means, 'I know your Name: It is "YHWH is the God
who acts with graciousness and mercy, the God who is
patient and acts with kindness and who extends reprieve
from punishment for as long as possible; but who must
finally resort to dealing with justice"'. If the Lord God were a
pharaoh of Egypt, his Name would be written like all royal
names, in the oval of a cartouche. Since mercy is a part of
God's very Name, Jonah knows how the Lord will respond
to Nineveh's repentance. And, 'It's not fair!' laments the
prophet. Rather it should be, 'Not Thy will but mine be
done!' is Jonah's outraged response.

This is like Jesus' parable of the workers in the vineyard.

For the kingdom of heaven is like a landowner who went
out early in the morning to hire labourers for his vineyard.
After agreeing with the labourers for the usual daily wage,
he sent them into his vineyard. When he went out about nine
o'clock, he saw others standing idle in the marketplace; and
he said to them, 'You also go into the vineyard, and I will
pay you whatever is right.' So they went. When he went out
again about noon and about three o'clock, he did the same.

4 Exod. 34:5–8. This same use of God's Name is to be found in Num.
14:18; Neh. 9:17; Ps. 86:15; 103:8; 145:8; 16:32; Joel 2:13; Jon. 4:2;
and Nah. 1:3.

And about five o'clock he went out and found others standing around; and he said to them, 'Why are you standing here
idle all day?' They said to him, 'Because no one has hired
us.' He said to them, 'You also go into the vineyard.' When
evening came, the owner of the vineyard said to his
manager, 'Call the labourers and give them their pay, beginning with the last and then going to the first'. When those
hired about five o'clock came, each of them received the
usual daily wage. Now when the first came, they thought
they would receive more; but each of them also received the
usual daily wage. And when they received it, they grumbled
against the landowner, saying, 'These last worked only one
hour, and you have made them equal to us who have borne
the burden of the day and the scorching heat.' But he replied
to one of them, 'Friend, I am doing you no wrong; did you
not agree with me for the usual daily wage? Take what
belongs to you and go; I choose to give to this last the
same as I give to you. Am I not allowed to do what I choose
with what belongs to me? Or are you jealous because I am
generous?'[5]

God's generosity and his mercy are not to be constricted by
our selfish notions of 'fairness', especially when that 'fairness' is usually directed for ourselves alone. We are indeed
like spoiled children and find it hard to grow up; we are
jealous because God is generous – to others. And St Paul
reminds us of that generosity of God when he says:

Indeed, rarely will anyone die for a righteous person –
though perhaps for a good person someone might actually
dare to die. But God proves his love for us in that while we
still were sinners Christ died for us.[6]

---

5 Matt. 20:1–15. For a lovely exposition of this and many others of
  Jesus' parables, see Charles W. F. Smith, (Philadelphia: United
  Church Press, *The Jesus of the Parables*: 1975), and especially the
  chapter, 'A Wideness in God's Mercy'.
6 Rom. 5:7–8.

IV. 3 *And now, O Lord, please take my life from me, for it is better for me to die than to live.*

How passionate is Jonah for his rights and his childlike sense of what be believes to be fair! He values his notion of 'justice' over life itself and would rather die than live in a world with a God who does not respect his 'rights'. His anger is really a blind rage that obscures even reason and in this he is like a self-indulgent child having a temper tantrum. While Cain's rage at his brother was murderous, Jonah's anger at God is self-destructive. We recall again the parable of Job and Job's own anger at the unfairness of his lot suggested by his three friends:

> Let the day perish in which I was born, and the night that said, 'A man-child is conceived'. Why did I not die at birth, come forth from the womb and expire?[7]

Insofar as both Job and Jonah are parables trying to make sense of the overthrow of Israel and Judah by Assyria and Babylon, we have to admire the courage which is able to parody its own childish tantrum. Here is a self-insight rare in our own day and in our modern institutions, whether political or religious. The reduction of our insignificant and selfish foibles to comic characterization would seem to be a most wholesome exercise. Yet we persist in taking our imagined liberties and rights so seriously as to become myopic in the matter of God's plan for his universe!

IV. 4 *And the Lord said, 'Is it right for you to be angry?'*

At first it would seem that the Lord is laughing at Jonah and his outburst; but reading again we might understand this verse as: 'How dare you be angry?' or 'What right do you have to be angry?' Perhaps it is a little of both – the Lord's

---

7 Job 3:3,11.

amusement at Jonah's fulminations, and God's pique at Jonah's intransigence. Certainly it is a less fearsome approach than he uses with Job when he reveals himself in the great whirlwind and demands that Job give an account of himself and his demands for his rights. We may be sure that there is a limit to God's patience with his people when they drag their feet in his service.

It is interesting to note that once the people of Nineveh have repented, God must return to the task of calling his own chosen servants to repentance. Jesus calls attention to this paradox when he says:

> This generation is a wicked generation; it looks for a sign, but no sign will be given to it except the sign of Jonah. For just as Jonah became a sign to the people of Nineveh, so the Son of Man will be a sign to this generation. The queen of the South will rise up at the judgement with the people of this generation and condemn them, because she came from the ends of the earth to hear the wisdom of Solomon – and now, something greater than Solomon is here! The people of Nineveh will stand up at the judgement with this generation and condemn it, because they repented when Jonah preached to them – and now, something greater than Jonah is here![8]

In using the words 'is it right', the Lord uses a form of the word 'the Good'; 'Are you doing "the Good" by being angry?' We are reminded of the general rule given to Cain in his jealousy and anger: 'If you do the Good, you are always acceptable to me; if you do not do the Good, SIN is waiting to devour you'. Be careful, Jonah, lest your anger and jealousy lead you to the same action as Cain took against his brother Abel. Perhaps we should call God's question to Jonah a gentle but firm warning, as Jesus warned the men of his generation who delighted in their own chosenness as the children of Abraham:

8 Luke 11:29–32.

> Therefore produce fruit that proves your repentance, and
> don't begin to say to yourselves, 'We have Abraham as our
> father'. For I tell you that God can raise up children for
> Abraham from these stones![9]

We dare not forget that Jesus, on one occasion, called Peter
the first Pope: 'Satan'. Implicit in Jonah's obsession with
himself and his sense of fairness expressed in his anger we
hear echoed Cain's unconcerned retort to the Lord's question concerning the whereabouts of his brother: 'Am I my
brother's keeper?'

IV. 5 *Then Jonah went out of the city and sat down east of the city, and made a booth for himself there. He sat under it in the shade, waiting to see what would become of the city.*

Verses 5–8 are a small parable within the larger one of
Jonah's mission. This parable within a parable will be used
in a 'from the lesser to the greater' teaching, or 'punch line',
in verses 9 and 10 at the very end.

Nineveh
City Wall & Gates

Does Jonah's sitting in the
east indicate that he began his
journey through the city at the
western gate and continued on
through to the other side?
Perhaps we can imagine that he
made his way out through the
gate dedicated to the Assyrian
god of the sun, the Shemesh (or
Shamash = the sun) Gate, and
there he undertakes to build a
shelter for himself from the sun.
The Hebrew word for the booth
which he builds is *succah*,
which is a kind of booth that
the pilgrims to Jerusalem build

9 Luke 3:8.

on the great Feast of Tabernacles, the wedding feast of God and his people mentioned earlier. When Jonah builds it in Nineveh, it is a poignant recollection of the temple of his native land which lies in ruins because of the Assyrians.

The function of the *succah* was in some fashion to remind the people of their journey through the wilderness before they came into the Land of Promise, and of the origins of their relationship with their God. The actual structure is quite temporary and must have a latticed covering, so that while sleeping in it during the eight days of the Feast one is able to see the stars. It is to be decorated with boughs and hanging fruits of the autumn. Symbolically it has connections also with the fertility of the earth, the rains (for which prayers are offered) and the sun itself.[10]

As the people of Israel lived 'on the move' in the wilderness, so the Lord had his own tabernacle which moved with the people. In the Promised Land the tabernacle of the Lord became permanent just as the people lived in permanent homes rather than the temporary structures of the wilderness. When the homes of the people of Israel were destroyed by Nineveh, God's home was destroyed as well:

> He has broken down his booth like that of a garden, laid in ruins the place of his appointed feasts; the Lord has brought an end in Zion to appointed feast and sabbath, and in his fierce indignation has spurned king and priest.[11]

> And daughter Zion is left like a booth in a vineyard, like a shelter in a cucumber field, like a besieged city.[12]

Another interpretation of this imagery of the booth is possible. The gardener responsible for a vineyard lived in a tempo-

10 For a fairly exhaustive description of the Feast of Tabernacles and its related institutions (like the *succah*), see D. Peter Burrows, 'The Feast of Sukkoth in Rabbinic and Related Literature', unpubl. dissertation (Hebrew Union College – Jewish Institute of Religion, Cincinnati, Ohio: 1974).

11 Lam. 2:6.

12 Isa. 1:8.

rary booth in the vineyard so that he might be better able to care for the vines and bring them to fruition and harvest. So in the beginning God set Adam, humankind, in his vineyard to 'till it and to cultivate it' and thus serve the Owner. But if the gardener loiters and takes his ease in the booth and refuses to serve in the vineyard, what good is he? Jesus himself is adamant of the need for working in the vineyard and producing much fruit from God's vineyard of the world.

But Jonah has not built this booth to rejoice in the Lord's creation and blessings or to remember the Lord's dwelling on earth; nor is he keen for nurturing the vineyard which is Nineveh. Rather he builds his booth as a shelter from the sun so that he can sit, take his ease and nurse his anger at the Lord in a great sulk, thumb in mouth. He also waits to see if the Lord might, after all, destroy the city of Nineveh. He is waiting for the Lord, but not to serve; rather, to bewail his own lot and indulge his 'righteous' anger. Poor, pitiful Jonah!

IV. 6   *The Lord God appointed a castor-oil plant, and made it come up over Jonah, to give shade over his head, to save him from his ill-humour; so Jonah was very happy about the castor-oil plant.*

At this point the Lord adds insult to injury – but oh so sweetly. He gives Jonah much-needed shade from the sun shining on the city, the Tigris River and the little booth. The exact translation of the plant is unclear. Some versions call it a vine, which is suggestive of the vintners' booth just mentioned. Others call it a 'shrub' or 'bush', reminiscent of the humble weed through which God had a conversation with the prophet Moses, the 'most humble man on earth'; such a contrast with Jonah whose national pride and prejudice has rendered him inert! The 'castor-oil plant' recommends itself for several reasons.[13] First, it is a fast grower in

---

13 As a child in the pre-resort era of Palm Springs, California, my family had a castor-oil plant by the front door of the shack on the Indian

the desert; second, it has huge leaves which give much shade; and finally, because of the oil of its fruit. Certainly Jonah needs a good dose of castor oil to move him into action! Scripture loves this earthy kind of humour. And we must remember that God loves to act through the humble and insignificant things.

It is important that we take note that it is the Lord who decorates the booth and makes his erstwhile servant comfortable, indulging Jonah's evil humour. Scripture uses the word 'appointed' to show that God and not some accident of a blown seed is responsible for the plant. 'There, there Jonah; take a nice spoon of castor-oil, lie down in the shade and take it easy', says the Lord. The Lord's clear intent is to save Jonah from himself and restore his servant to productivity. Jonah, apparently without much thought – or gratitude – enjoys the shade of the plant greatly.

IV. 7 *But when dawn came up the next day, God appointed a worm that attacked the castor-oil plant, so that it withered.*

'Easy come, easy go' is the phrase that springs to mind about the castor-oil plant and its wonderful shade. No gratitude, no shade! And as the Lord 'appointed' the castor-oil plant, so now he 'appoints' the worm, which has not just accidentally wandered in upon the plant either. 'The Lord gives; and the Lord takes away' – and don't you forget it, Jonah!

The worm, like the castor-oil plant it attacks, is a nice touch. Low creature on the animal totem pole, the worm, like the locust, consumes and destroys without being productive. Jonah and the worm have much in common in the desire to consume without offering productivity. We are reminded of Isaiah's homily on the Lord's intent to restore

reservation in the Mojave Desert where we lived. I spent many hours sitting in its shade; it is a remarkable and beautiful shade plant indeed, growing in sand!

his people from their exile:

> Do not fear, you worm Jacob, you insect Israel! I will help
> you, says the Lord; your Redeemer is the Holy One of
> Israel.[14]

Here is a remarkable and parabolic worm, much like that
great worm leviathan and the first, four-legged worm which
inhabited the Tree of Knowledge in the Garden of Eden.
This worm is set loose by the Lord at dawn, before the
desert heat begins, so that Jonah finds himself in exactly the
same situation in which he began his vigil on the city.

IV. 8 *When the sun rose, God prepared a sultry east wind, and the sun beat down on the head of Jonah so that he was faint and asked that he might die. He said, 'It is better for me to die than to live.'*

God has not finished with his appointment of things for
Jonah. Like the plagues of Egypt, one follows the other to
give a cumulative effect, on the principle of 'if that were not
bad enough, God now appoints yet another' discomfort for
Jonah. This one is the sultry east wind off the desert, like
the wind from the Mojave Desert in California called the
'Santana' and the wind which blows off the Sahara Desert
over Europe, called the Sirocco. Of the Santana, Raymond
Chandler wrote in a short story called 'Red Wind'
published in 1938 in *Black Mask Magazine*:

> Those hot dry winds that come down through the mountain
> passes and curl your hair and make your nerves jump and
> your skin itch. On nights like that every booze party ends in
> a fight. Meek little wives feel the edge of the carving knife
> and study their husbands' necks. Anything can happen.

Jonah has been hot under the collar; now the Lord moves

14 Isa. 41:14.

the heat to his head and bakes him. Perhaps Jonah was expecting fire from heaven to fall on Nineveh as the Lord had caused the fire from heaven to fall on the wicked city of Sodom. But the fire of the sun fell on Jonah instead, so that he felt faint.

Once again Jonah contemplates and entertains death: 'I'm so hot I could die!' As once he begged for death to relieve himself of the heat of his own anger, so now the source of his discomfort is God's doing, God's own righteous indignation at Jonah's intractability, and Jonah begs for death.

Jonah invokes his perception of the Good again: 'It would be the Good for me to die.' But God's Good established at the creation itself is so much greater than Jonah's puny 'the good for me'. God will now counter with his Good for his whole creation, as at the beginning. 'I want my world back, and you, Jonah, are to get it back for me. That is your mission and I am tired of dealing with your petty claims for your rights! Get up and go, Jonah!'

How often does the Church stew in the heat of its own privileges, and claim its own selfish concerns for self-definition and the rights of this group or that within it. Navelgazing ecumenism and the proprieties of ordination of this one or that look so much like Jonah, asleep in the hold of the boat or stewing in the juices of his own concerns in his little booth outside the city walls. What worm or locust will God appoint to destroy the comforting shade? God is patient indeed – but not forever. The harvest is plentiful, but the labourers are few enough for them to be so busy with their own nit-picking concerns and their own little 'goods for me'.

This marks the end of the 'parable within a parable'. And now for the dénouement.

IV. 9 *But God said to Jonah, 'Is it (the) Good for you to be angry about the castor-oil plant?' And he said, 'Yes, angry enough to die'.*

The Lord begins to set up the terms of the 'from the lesser to the greater' argument.

Jonah's definition of the Good is to care so profoundly for the castor-oil plant (though he did not make it) that the loss of it causes him to be angry enough to offer to die. For him the Good is 'the good life' and what is 'fair', and he is not best pleased with the loss of either of the plant or his 'rights' to enjoy it. In short, he would even give his life and is possessed of an extraordinary passion – or compassion – for the castor-oil plant which grew in a night and disappeared in a night. Clearly he loves the shade-giving plant and his right to it as much as, if not more than his own life! So we must understand the plant in the larger sense of all the goodness and comfort which the Lord had given his people, including the temple where God lived among his people. Their anger over the 'unfairness' of the Lord's permitting it all to be destroyed by the Ninevites, which the people interpret as being the Lord's favouritism to Nineveh, is enormous and blinding. They cannot see God's larger purpose of mission because of their jealousy of the 'good-for-nothing' Assyrians.

IV. 10 *Then the Lord said, 'You are concerned about the bush, for which you did not labour and which you did not grow; it came into being in a night and perished in a night.*

The Lesser: If your passion for the plant which you did not create, which gave you comfort and ease while you sat fulminating about the fate of Nineveh and what seemed righteous to you, is so great that you would give your life for the castor-oil plant ...

IV. 11 *And should I not show mercy to Nineveh, that great city, in which there are more than a hundred and twenty thousand persons who do not know their right hand from their left, and also many animals?'*

The Greater: ... then how much more my passion and compassion for this great city which I did create and which is a part of my whole creation in which I take great pleasure and for which I would override my own certainty of what is fair and righteous to show mercy. After all, part of my Name is: 'The Lord who is gracious and extends mercy'. Perhaps Nineveh is even worth a life, but it is certainly worth enough to give up that justice which is so profoundly important to me and upon which the whole creation is founded, to save it!

Notice that Nineveh is not only the huge population (for the time) of 120,000 human souls, but also the animal lives which are dependent upon Nineveh. That these 120,000 folks do not know right hand from left indicates that they are truly children despite their sophistication as a great culture of the time. Perhaps it is because they are children they find it easier to repent, for Jesus says of them later:

> The people of Nineveh will rise up at the judgment with this generation and condemn it, because they repented at the proclamation of Jonah, and see, something greater than Jonah is here![15]

Except you become as a little child, totally dependent because you do not know your right hand from your left, you cannot enter the Kingdom of Heaven.

If the Book of Jonah were an historical book, we might expect the story to continue; what happened to Nineveh after all? where did Jonah go from his booth after his conversation with God? how did the king of Nineveh and

15 Luke 11:32.

his nobles implement their repentance into their daily lives? The fact that Jonah ends so abruptly with God's question to Jonah and with no answer from the prophet is indicative that our story is a parable, the point of which parable lies in God's proclamation of his intention of saving the repentant sinners of Nineveh, never mind Jonah's objections. And as a parable, the story is always and everywhere true. It can apply to the Church in our present time and the Church's belief about its status as the elect and chosen people of God just as much as it applied to Israel as God's chosen in Jonah's time. Chosenness by God is always election for service, never for special and most-favoured treatment.

God's intentions are ever clear: he wants his world back, a world alienated from him by sin; his chosen people are commissioned to get the world back for him – whatever the cost to themselves. And when the elect look more to their own protection, preservation and rights and privileges, they are asleep in the hold of the boat while all hell is breaking loose in the world and its people are scared to death.

Chapter Five

The Book of the Prophet Nahum is entitled: 'An oracle concerning Nineveh. The Book of the vision of Nahum of Elkosh.' While Nahum also addresses Nineveh as Jonah has been called to do, so different is his prophecy from that of Jonah that I have chosen to ignore him until this chapter of summary in order to use his prophecy as a comparison to Jonah's.

The overarching context for Jonah's prophecy is the Name of God, which we have identified as his behavioural qualities – his inclinations. In Jonah God is portrayed as having the twofold inclinations of justice (including the punishment for injustice) and mercy (an aberration of and offence against justice). Jonah opens with the Lord's judgement on Nineveh: 'Their wickedness stares me in the face', and a strong implication of the punishment that will befall Nineveh if it keeps to its present course. The chaos before the creation is portrayed by the great storm, the hell which breaks loose as a result of the rejection of God's creative and sustaining Word – the Good.

Yet while this righteous anger of the Lord is portrayed in Jonah by only half of a single verse, we find the following in Nahum:

A jealous and avenging God is the Lord, the Lord is avenging and wrathful; the Lord takes vengeance on his adversaries and rages against his enemies. The Lord is slow to
anger but great in power, and the Lord will by no means
clear the guilty. His way is in whirlwind and storm, and the
clouds are the dust of his feet. He rebukes the sea and makes
it dry, and he dries up all the rivers; Bashan and Carmel
wither, and the bloom of Lebanon fades. The mountains
quake before him, and the hills melt; the earth heaves before
him, the world and all who live in it. Who can stand before
his indignation? Who can endure the heat of his anger? His
wrath is poured out like fire, and by him the rocks are
broken in pieces. The Lord is good, a stronghold in a day of
trouble; he protects those who take refuge in him, even in a
rushing flood. He will make a full end of his adversaries,
and will pursue his enemies into darkness. Why do you plot
against the Lord? He will make an end; no adversary will
rise up twice. Like thorns they are entangled, like drunkards
they are drunk; they are consumed like dry straw. From you
one has gone out who plots evil against the Lord, one who
counsels wickedness. Thus says the Lord, 'Though they are
at full strength and many, they will be cut off and pass
away. Though I have afflicted you, I will afflict you no
more. And now I will break off his yoke from you and snap
the bonds that bind you.' The Lord has commanded
concerning you: 'Your name shall be perpetuated no longer;
from the house of your gods I will cut off the carved image
and the cast image. I will make your grave, for you are
worthless'.[1]

This judgement of God delivered to Nineveh resembles
more a ton of bricks, and the inclination of the Lord
towards mercy seems completely missing here. There is, as
a part of Nahum's prophecy, a statement of God's mercy,
but it is a mercy reserved only for Israel:

Look! On the mountains the feet of one who brings good
tidings, who proclaims peace! Celebrate your festivals, O

---

1   Nahum 1:2-14.

Judah, fulfill your vows, for never again shall the wicked invade you; they are utterly cut off. A shatterer has come up against you [Nineveh]. Guard the ramparts; watch the road; gird your loins; collect all your strength. (For the Lord is restoring the Pride of Jacob, as well as the Majesty of Israel, though ravagers have ravaged them and ruined their branches.)[2]

According to Nahum, Judah (Jacob) and Israel's chosen status is to be restored to them if they will but hold on. Their chosenness is a given and has no purpose, whereas in Jonah we have seen that Judah and Israel have been chosen for service in the enterprise of God's mission to get his world back for himself.

For Nahum Nineveh is the enemy of God's people who will be destroyed in God's righteous anger at them, while in Jonah Nineveh is the object of the Lord's desire as a part of his beloved creation – sheep of his flock who have wandered away. Nahum preaches revenge, not repentance.

We have spoken of national pride and its concomitant national prejudice against the outsider as a major obstacle to Israel's function as the servant of God, in business to sacrifice pride and work in great humility under the Lord's Kingship to restore the Gentiles to his fold. Nahum's promise to restore pride and majesty to the chosen ones at the expense of the Gentiles – here Nineveh – seems to be the direct opposite from the mission of Jonah. Nahum promises vengeance against Nineveh and the restoration of Israel to the *status quo ante bellum*. The instrument of God to destroy the Ninevites is called 'the shatterer' and is probably the Medes and Babylonians threatening the city of Nineveh.

While the weakness of Nineveh might be the source of the fear which moves the Ninevites to repentance in Jonah, this same weakness is viewed by Nahum as the opportunity for their destruction and the restoration of the conquered

2 Nahum 1:15–2:2.

Israel. God's Name, 'the Lord, gracious and merciful', will never be made known to Nineveh by Nahum. They will die in their arrogance – and good riddance too!

Here is what Nineveh can expect from Israel's God, who loves only his own, by Nahum's reckoning:

> Devastation, desolation, and destruction! Hearts faint and knees tremble, all loins quake, all faces grow pale! What became of the lions' den, the cave of the young lions, where the lion goes, and the lion's cubs, with no one to disturb them? The lion has torn enough for his whelps and strangled prey for his lionesses; he has filled his caves with prey and his dens with torn flesh. See, I am against you, says the Lord of hosts, and I will burn your chariots in smoke, and the sword shall devour your young lions; I will cut off your prey from the earth, and the voice of your messengers shall be heard no more.[3]

The reading of Jonah as a parable of the meaning of the Exile of Israel from its land and temple, in order to move the slumbering servant of God into action and into mission, is totally missing from Nahum. In fact, there is no explanation for the Exile at all and no attempt to understand the meaning of it from the Lord's point of view. Nahum leaves us to see the overthrow of Israel by Nineveh as a kind of 'glitch' in the Lord's most-favoured-nation treatment of his chosen. 'Those nasty, old Ninevites crept in and stole my people while I wasn't looking; but do I ever mean to show them they can't get away with it!' is what Nahum would have us assume to be God's attitude.

Where the Lord's compassion is stirred for the rulers of Nineveh, 'the king and his nobles', by their repentance, Nahum's judgment on these rulers is rough indeed:

> Your shepherds are asleep, O king of Assyria; your nobles slumber. Your people are scattered on the mountains with no one to gather them. There is no assuaging your hurt,

3 Nahum 2:10–13.

your wound is mortal. All who hear the news about you clap their hands over you. For who has ever escaped your endless cruelty?[4]

Nahum's prophetic inclusion in the Canon of Scripture assures us that he is not reckoned to be one of the false prophets. However, we are tempted to believe that he is perhaps one of the more prosaic of prophets. His vision is limited in that he interprets events surrounding the fall of Nineveh to Babylon as the vindication of the Lord's justice towards his people. His prophecy for Israel is really: 'See! If you wait long enough, the Lord will restore what is "fair" for you and will restore your fortunes.' Nahum's acquaintance with God never discerns the much larger picture of the Lord's desire for all peoples of the world to return to him. Nahum's vision is popular religion: the good are rewarded if only they persist while the evil are most assuredly punished. What goes around, comes around; swings and roundabouts.

Jonah's prophecy is a more transcendent, even mystical religion. It contains the notion of sacrifice and a hard-won humility before the greater will and purposes of God, of which notions Nahum is utterly devoid. While Jonah at the outset of the parable shares some of the same prejudices against Nineveh that characterize Nahum's fulminations, the parable moves to a repentance of the prophet which permits of his uttering the high priestly formula: 'Take me, bind me, and throw me overboard' and of offering his life for the salvation of foreigners and outsiders.

We suggested in chapter one that Jesus' identification of himself with Jonah and the sign of Jonah is through the title 'Son of Man':

For just as Jonah was three days and three nights in the belly of the sea monster, so for three days and three nights the Son of Man will be in the heart of the earth.[5]

4 Nahum 3:18–19.
5 Matt. 12:40.

While this title, when it is used as God's address to his prophet Ezekiel, is really no title at all but simply another way of referring to Ezekiel as a 'mortal man', I would suggest that when Jesus uses it about himself, which he does frequently, he does so with Jonah in mind. And when Jesus thinks of Jonah, he thinks of Jonah's offering of his life for the salvation of Gentiles. Jesus apprehends Jonah as Jonah the sacrifice, Jonah the suffering servant. This is quite clear in his teaching to his disciples:

> ... for he was teaching his disciples, saying to them, 'The Son of Man is to be betrayed into human hands, and they will kill him, and three days after being killed, he will rise again.'[6]

The word 'betrayed' is the same sacrificial word 'bound over' which we saw first in the story of the 'Binding of Isaac' in Genesis 22. When he says he (the Son of Man) will be 'killed', it is the sacrificial word for the slaughter or dispatch of the sacrificial victim, the lamb for God. Just as the sacrifice of the lamb for God was, in fact, the offering by the High Priest of his own life so that Israel might be delivered of Sin, so I believe that Jesus saw Jonah – and himself – as a kind of High Priest for the nations which, though they might very well repent, had no means of paying the ultimate price for reconciliation with God as Israel did, no one to say to the Lord: 'Take my life in the stead of theirs'.

Certainly this concept is miles away from anything that Nahum believed about Nineveh, about Israel and about himself and his own role in God's purposes for his world. Nahum is more like the pre-crucifixion disciples in their misapprehension of Jesus' purposes as being the restoration of the glory of the Kingdom of Israel: 'And they said to him, "Grant us to sit, one at your right hand and one at your left, in your glory."'[7] Sacrifice and self-offering make no sense

6 Mark 9:31.
7 Mark 10:37.

to them in the context of the defeat of the Romans and the restoration of an earthly kingdom and power. They see only the defeat of the power of Rome as the goal; they cannot yet wrap their minds around the sacrifice of Jesus for the salvation of Rome. Jesus attempts to teach them that God's intent for Rome is identical to his goal for Nineveh in the parable of Jonah.

So much depends upon our apprehension of our true goal and purpose as the chosen ones of God. Do we struggle to rule over the field or do we see only the harvest which is plentiful and needs to be gathered in? Do we view ourselves and our goals as having an ever higher and more important place in the hierarchy that rules over the institution, or as humble servants and missionaries compelled by the goal of the Owner of the field of the world who sacrifices his own love of justice in order to redeem that world in mercy for himself? Consider Jesus' constant teaching of the latter!

A rich young man comes to Jesus and asks: 'What must I do to inherit eternal life?' Jesus replies, 'You know the Ten Commandments.' 'Oh yes,' says the man, 'I am scrupulous in keeping them and always have been'.

> Jesus, looking at him, loved him and said, 'You lack one thing; go, sell what you own, and give the money to the poor, and you will have treasure in heaven; then come, follow me.' When he heard this, he was shocked and went away grieving, for he had many possessions.[8]

The mistake of this young man is that his goal for himself is eternal life, the great reward and payoff for being righteous. He is keeping his part of the bargain with God and expects the yield on his investment, i.e. the good are rewarded. Jesus' love for him seeks to move him beyond this practical transaction to the bigger picture of the will of God. 'Give up' or 'sacrifice' your hope for reward and all your other treasure which you value; there will be plenty of treasure in

8 Mark 10:21–2.

heaven – later. 'Come, follow me' in a life of humble service which will ultimately lead to the sacrifice of life itself – for others. Your reward will be the accomplishment of God's purpose and the salvation of sinners simply because God wants it.

This poor rich man cannot move from his hopes for heaven to a life of sacrificial mission. Yet he is like so many whose religion is based upon the hope for reward. It is easier, says the Lord, for one whose goal is the heavenly payoff to be a part of the Kingdom than for a camel to squeeze through the eye of a needle!

It is this shift of goals with which Jonah and Jesus in their turns confront us which Claude Montefiore describes in this way:

> This we may regard as a new, important and historic feature in his [Jesus'] teaching. And it is here that opposition comes in and begins. To call sinners to repentance, to denounce vice generally, is one thing. To have intercourse with sinners and seek their conversion by countenancing them and comforting them – that is quite another thing.[9]

And one is very tempted to add, to give one's very life for these sinners so that they may be delivered from the chaos and death which they fear is a further thing so incredible as to make the mind boggle.

Here is the true sign of Jonah – to be able to give up, to sacrifice that which is fair and just for oneself in order to extend God's mercy to those who clearly do not deserve it; to eat with publicans and sinners; to invite the terrified in the hells of the storms of this world to 'take me, and bind me, and throw me overboard' so that they may live and be safe though it cost me even my life.

This is truly thinking outside the box of ordinary religion; this is the sign of Jonah – to be a missionary, no matter how reluctant, not for any reward save the fulfil-

9 Claude G. Montefiore, *The Synoptic Gospels*, 1st edn. Vol. 1 (Macmillan, London and Basingstoke, 1927), p. lxxxv.

ment of the purpose of God, to the end that:

> On that day there shall be inscribed on the bells of the horses, 'Holy to the Lord'. And the cooking pots in the house of the Lord shall be as holy as the bowls in front of the altar; and every cooking pot in Jerusalem and Judah shall be sacred to the Lord of hosts, so that all who sacrifice may come and use them to boil the flesh of the sacrifice. And there shall no longer be traders [people called foreigners or gentiles] in the house of the Lord of hosts on that day [everybody and everything will be the Lord's own].
>
> And the Lord will become king over all the earth; on that day the Lord will be one and his name one [for all peoples].[10]

---

10 Zech. 14:20–1 and 14:9.

Printed in the United Kingdom
by Lightning Source UK Ltd.
133428UK00001B/91-213/P